TRANSIT TALK

TRANSIT TALK

NEW YORK'S BUS AND SUBWAY WORKERS
TELL THEIR STORIES

Robert W. Snyder

A Copublication of

THE NEW YORK TRANSIT MUSEUM
BROOKLYN, NEW YORK

and

RUTGERS UNIVERSITY PRESS
NEW BRUNSWICK, NEW JERSEY, AND LONDON

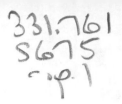

LIBRARY OF CONGRESS CATALOGING-IN-PUBLICATION DATA

Snyder, Robert W., 1955–
    Transit talk : New York's bus and subway workers tell their
stories / Robert W. Snyder.
        p.   cm.
    Includes bibliographical references and index.
    ISBN 0-8135-2576-4 (cloth : alk. paper). — ISBN 0-8135-2577-2
(pbk. : alk. paper)
    1. Transport workers—New York (State)—New York—
Anecdotes.   2. Bus drivers—New York (State)—New York—
Anecdotes. 3. Subways—New York (State)—New York.
4. Bus lines—New York (State)—New York.   5. New York
City Transit Authority—Officials and employees.   I. Title.
HD8039.T72U466   1998
331.7'61388'09747—dc21   98-7049
                                                                   CIP

British Cataloging-in-Publication data for this book is available from
the British Library

Interior Design: JUDITH MARTIN WATERMAN

Manufactured in the United States of America

To my grandfather,

Emil A. Ossmann,

a New York City transit worker from
October 16, 1918, to February 12, 1966

CONTENTS

NOTES FROM UNDERGROUND

PETE HAMILL

In memory, I am with my brother Tom on a hot morning in August and we are riding the Brighton Beach line. We are navigating the terrain of Brooklyn, through tunnels, into open cuts, up on the elevated rails. The rhythm is always the same: from darkness to light. We are peering from the front window of the first car, the steel rails extending into the darkness, with mysterious lights of warning and welcome telling us that there are paths here we cannot know. And then a way off, we can see the light of day, and then suddenly there are plump bushes of roses cascading over the tops of concrete walls, and flowers we are still too young and too urban to name. Birds rise in flocks at the sound of the train. We can see an old Italian man tending a fig tree. Climbing higher onto a stretch of old elevated tracks, we can glimpse lives of strangers through tenement windows. And then up ahead, a giant brightness, is the sea.

I don't remember much about the other passengers. Surely many were like us: kids bound for the ocean on a hot summer morning. But for Tom and me, what mattered was the ride, the great roar through the tunnels and gardens of Brooklyn, the feel of power and destination. And at the end of the ride, the adventurous sands of the great city beach.

The Brighton Beach line wasn't the only subway for us, of

course; we had to walk a long way to get to it. But it was the most varied and surprising. And we were driven by curiosity. Here we were in this immense city, and most of the time we were confined to our own small hamlet in Brooklyn. The subway was our ticket to places as different and exotic as foreign countries. Sometimes, when we were very young, our mother would take us to some of those places: to Times Square and Orchard Street, to Herald Square and the distant Bronx. The world was full of marvels. There were Chinese people and Jewish people, people who spoke Spanish and others who spoke Italian, people from Poland and people from Russia and people whose ancestors had come from Africa. Sometimes we were visiting relatives, other immigrants from Ireland and their children. But often, the purpose of our journeys was sheer pleasure. Anne Devlin Hamill was showing her children that the whole city was theirs, and that within its five boroughs, you could find the world. It was only a subway ride away.

There was no beginning to my consciousness of the subway; it was always there. I was on the subway with my parents before I could read. And that meant that there was never any fear attached to using it. From the beginning, the subway gave us access to the glories of Manhattan. In my part of Brooklyn, we always said we were going "over New York" (never, as people in Queens said, "to the City"), a throwback, I suppose, to the days when Brooklyn was an independent city. I remember once going to Times Square with my brother Tom and seeing the great featherweight champion, Willie Pep, walking in the company of a blond woman who towered over him by at least a foot. He was the first celebrity we had ever seen and we followed him for three blocks and then sighed in disappointment when he led the giant woman through the revolving doors of the Hotel Taft.

In my early teens, I took the subway every morning from Brooklyn to my high school in upper Manhattan. The journey required three different trains. I boarded the F at Seventh Avenue, and leaned against a door as it rose out of the tunnel at Fourth Avenue to climb the high trestle over the Gowanus Canal, stopping at Smith-Ninth, then Carroll Street and Bergen

Street before screeching into Jay Street–Borough Hall. There I crossed to the A train of Duke Ellington and Billy Strayhorn, all shiny and new in those years right after World War II. I held on for the deep rushing plunge under the river. I changed again two stops later at Broadway-Nassau, leaping up stairs two at a time to the Fulton Street station, afraid of missing a connection and losing precious minutes, part of a galloping time-tortured crowd. And then boarded the Lexington Avenue Express.

I loved the Lexington Avenue Express. These were the oldest trains in the city, with meshed-straw benches running along each side, seated passengers burying their faces in the morning tabloids, those who were seatless holding onto the horizontal bars or vertical poles, swaying back and forth, and still more clustered in the dark blocky spaces at the end of each car. The Lexington Avenue Express sometimes made me feel that I'd entered a time machine and if I got off at Fourteenth Street I would emerge in the New York of 1912. The express had immense power, fed by 600 volts from the third rail, and the stretch from Grand Central to Eighty-sixth Street was one of the greatest rides in the entire system. The train simply roared, whizzing past local trains and local stations, the girders going by too quickly to count, the combined roar of train and tunnel sounding like triumph.

In the evening, the ride had a different quality. Passengers read afternoon newspapers, the *Post*, the *World-Telegram*, the *Journal-American*, and often seemed drained or beaten by the day. In those years, New York was still a blue-collar town and in those evening trains there was always a salty aroma of sweat. Working men with grizzled faces and blackened nails were heading home to hot baths and dinner tables. They wore rough clothes and heavy steel-tipped workmen's boots. Some had tool belts lashed to their waists. At Fulton Street, many young women came into the trains from the offices of Wall Street and the workmen gazed at them in a longing way. Sometimes they spoke awkwardly to each other. A young woman would smile. A workman would bow. And months later you would see them traveling together in the mornings.

In the mornings, we were all ruled by the metronome of the

clock. We arrived at the station at the same time and caught the same trains. After a while, the man in the change booth became more than a pair of hands. He acquired a face and then a name and soon there were words of greeting and luck. The same was true with the conductors. Some had personalities and a line of gab; others were dour and withdrawn. We never got to see the motormen. But we were joined, twice a day, in the great railroad of New York.

ⅢⅢ

It was hard to imagine, growing up with the subway, that there was a time when human beings actually feared the places beneath the skin of the earth. And yet this has been the case all the way back to the years before written history. From the Celts to the Maya, from Africa to Asia, there have been myths of the Underworld. It is the place of eternal damnation or a country of banished gods, awaiting their return to the surface. It is the holding pen of evil spirits. In some versions, it contains a second world, filled with lakes and streams and creatures of immense intelligence; that idyllic vision is rare. Usually, the entrance is through a cave or a cleft in the earth and most of the time the entrance leads to Hell. Virgil, born in 70 B.C., took us there in the Aeneid; thirteen centuries later, Dante followed him into the Inferno from which all pity had been erased.

In the nineteenth century, fear of the unknown was part of the debate about driving subways under the surface of cities. Some fundamentalist Christians spoke darkly about violating the will of God. They thundered from pulpits. They wrote letters to newspapers. But as population soared in the cities of Europe and the United States, and engineering became more sophisticated, the subway became inevitable. The invention in 1818 by Marc Isambard Brunel of the tunneling shield, and its use in the building of a tunnel under the Thames, meant that subway tunnels could be built in cities with spongy subsoils. Work on that first London tunnel was completed in 1859. In the process, men died, learning a brand-new skill in places where no men had ever been. That first tunnel was to be used by horse-drawn vehicles and pedestrian traffic. But the next logical step was a subway. Money was raised. Work began. The

Underground opened in London on January 10, 1863, the first to appear anywhere on earth.

Combining tunnels and open cuts, the London subway used steam locomotives to haul passengers 3.7 miles. There were problems with ventilation, noxious fumes, nauseating odors; nevertheless, the expansion of the system continued. It would take until 1890 before the lines were electrified. And then systems were built elsewhere: Budapest (1896), Paris (1900), Berlin (1902). In all these places, technology was refined, experience gained. And engineers worked to make the experience more pleasant, lighting station platforms, ornamenting them with tiles and art, trying to take ancient fears out of this version of the underworld.

Through all of this, New York lagged far behind. The reasons were familiar: politics and greed. In the years after the Civil War, Tammany Hall boss William Marcy Tweed opposed all suggestions about building a subway. The city's population was to increase fivefold in twenty years; a million horses turned the streets into foul avenues, slippery with horse dung in the rain, the air filled with flaking fecal matter on dry days. Still, the Boss was opposed. He insisted that subways were impractical. This probably meant that he didn't want a system from which he could not extort his piece of the action. Whatever his motive, he threw his support to a system of elevated trains.

In Tweed's heyday, a brilliant man named Alfred Ely Beach set out to prove Tweed wrong. A former editor of the *New York Sun*, Beach was editor and co-owner of *Scientific American*, and a friend of most of the era's finest inventors and engineers. In 1869, Beach decided to build a subway in secret, only hundreds of feet from City Hall. He directed the building of a tunnel under Broadway between Warren Street and Park Place. He had a permit to build a pneumatic mail tube, but he secretly made it much larger. Tons of earth were moved through the basement of Devlin's Clothing Store at the corner of Warren Street. And in February 1870, the first New York subway was opened for demonstrations. It traveled only 312 feet and was pneumatically powered (by a huge fan called the Western Tornado). But by all accounts it was a lovely thing to see: frescoes adorned the platform, along with a fountain and plush chairs and a man playing a grand piano.

But plans to go ahead with a true subway were vetoed by the state's governor, who was controlled by the enraged Tweed. New York City was soon marred by the ugly structures of elevated trains. The secret subway of Alfred Beach was eventually sealed and forgotten. In 1897, Boston opened the first American subway, using trolley cars that were soon electrified. New York didn't get its first subway until October 27, 1904, when the IRT began service from City Hall to 145th Street. It was an immediate success and other lines were soon under construction.

The subways changed the city. They pushed into the Bronx and deep into Brooklyn and allowed hundreds of thousands of people to settle in more bucolic places and still get to work on time. Communities in those outer boroughs grew like towns in the West, following the railhead. The patterns of life in Manhattan also changed. Broadway merchants had gone to court to prevent the building of subways beneath their avenue, the most obvious route for this new kind of urban transportation. They feared damage to their buildings. They didn't want the disruptions of the open-trench style of building the tunnels (digging down from the surface and then roofing the tracks). So the first IRT ran up the East Side to what became Grand Central and then beyond. New department stores, located in the swiftly developing new midtown, soon eclipsed the smug downtown Broadway stores, which never recovered. Meanwhile, new lines were added throughout Manhattan. Harlem was built. The West Side expanded. The subways became the great linking system of New York, first knitting together all sections of Manhattan, then joining Brooklyn, Queens, and the Bronx to the greater city. They remain essential to the city today.

ⅢⅢ

Through all the years of its existence, most of us have taken the subway system for granted. It seems that it was always there and always would be. Only on the rare occasions of strikes do we realize how much it means to us. And it is only during strikes that most New Yorkers even think about the more than forty thousand men and women who make the system work.

They are the subject of this book. There is one quality present in almost all their stories: pride. They know that what they do is important, and they are proud of the parts they play in the great daily enterprise.

Many of them have come through dark days in the system. For too long a time, the subways justified ancient fears. Crime soared. Killers moved through the trains. Menacing groups of young men terrified older citizens. I remember watching the changes. Passengers no longer buried themselves in newspapers; they needed to be constantly alert to danger. Very few risked sleep. I stopped seeing women from Brooklyn and Queens carrying shopping bags from the department stores of Manhattan; the store labels on the bags were too often invitations to thieves. The saga of Bernie Goetz and the young men he shot in 1984 became a metaphor for the condition of the subways.

The men and women of the system lived through those awful days. Some retired in despair. Some died. There were periodic horror stories: token clerks torched in their booths, others shot after a robbery by hoodlums without mercy. Many came to work in a state of anxiety. Many had nightmares when they went home.

But they kept working. They kept doing their jobs. And now, with the century winding down, you can almost hear them sighing in relief. Crime is way down in New York City and is down even more in the subways. That is, today's passenger is even safer in the subway than he or she is in the streets. I was among those who had backed away from the system in the bad days; as a newspaperman I had covered too many horrors in those crumbling stations. But I use the trains every day now— O glorious MetroCard!—and the mood is very different. The token clerks are relaxed. The conductors are smiling. Passengers are relaxing into books and reading newspapers in several languages. Historians will have to decide who was responsible for giving the subways back to the citizens of New York. But they are now ours again and that is a wonderful thing indeed.

Safe or dangerous, the subways cannot exist without the men and women who are the heart of the system. And this also must be said: those men and women would not function as well without the Transport Workers Union, which fought for their dignity and well-being during many dark days. In most of these interviews, the union is a constant point of reference. The older men and women remember old struggles; the young have been the beneficiaries of those struggles. But it is clear that the union has strengthened the pride of the workers themselves and the system that they operate.

ⅢⅢⅢ

I don't know if kids today board the trains in a spirit of adventure. I hope they do. Those trains can give them the world, bring them to places where dozens of languages are spoken, where foods can be sampled from a hundred nations, where the shops play music that was born on the other side of the planet. New York is a city of many parishes that must never be parochial. The trains are an agency of exploration and mixture, a means of seeing the many places and people who make up the metropolis. The passengers themselves are symbols of that city. Some are going to work. Some are going to school. Some are going to visit the nation's grandest museums and finest theaters. Some, on hot August mornings, are going to the beach. All are riding into the limitless American future.

ACKNOWLEDGMENTS

The New York Transit Museum deserves thanks for sponsoring this book, which began as a project in folklore and oral history. The interviews that form the backbone of *Transit Talk* were conducted under the direction of City Lore, Inc. Most of the interviews cited were conducted by Joseph Sciorra and Sally Charnow. Additional interviews were by Steve Zeitlin, Ray Allen, and Susan Brophy. Their work gave this project a solid start. The greatest credit, however, goes to the people who generously shared their stories: Joseph Allotta, Ed Bagley, Raymond Berger, Jerry Bokino, Lionel Bostick, Earnis Briant, Richard Buffington, Carolyn Burke, Joe Caracciolo, Joe Cassar, Elena Chang, William Connor, Johnny Cox, James Daniels, Lionel Daniels, James Davitt, Joey Deher, Victor De Santo, Tom Diana, Arthur Ferguson, Joe Fernandez, Joseph P. Fox, Urias Fritz, Jean Frugone, Larry Furlong, A. R. Goodlatte, Victor H. Gordon Jr., Thomas Granger, David Gunn, Barbara Hand, Don Harold, Nelson Harris, George Havriliak, Brenda Hayes, Joe Hoffman, Floyd Holloway, Mildred Hunter, Ronny Johnson, Theodore Jones, Marty Kaiser, Robert Kolacz, Ed Krieger, Whitfield Lee, Diane Leibovitz, Carlos Lezama, Mike Lombardi, John Lorusso, Jenny Mandelino, Richard Marks, John Maye, Fred McFarland, Kevin McGarvey, Scotty McShane, Carol Meltzer, Wallace Mobley, Frances Murphy, Walter Noonan, Domingo Noriega, Harry Nugent, Richard Oakes, Leonard Offner, Hector Perez, Paul Prinzivalli, Vincent Ricciardelli, Emilio Robertino, Penny Rohls, Rosalyn Samuels,

Anthony Santella, William Scheiner, Eric Schmidt, Albert Schneider, Angela Sealy, Roland E. Shelton Sr., Edward Silberfarb, Charles E. Smith, Chuck Stanford, Stanley Stern, Joseph Tesoriero, Shirley Thaler, Richie Triolo, Lloyd Tyler, Jeffrey Van Clief, John Waddell, Jack Wheaton, Dan Whitty, Robert Williams, Chuck "The Wolf" the subway singer, Samuel Zelensky, and Dot Zionek.

In addition to these interviews, I asked questions of transit workers while I rode the bus and subway and also visited different sites in the transit system on my own. I thank both the anonymous transit workers who answered my questions and also my guides on my formal visits: at the Bergen Street Shop, Michael O'Halloran, Virginia McGeagh, Ronald Coleman, Keith Smith, Jose Alvarado, John Thompson; in the subway tunnels and elevated structures of Brooklyn, Joseph Quacinella; at the Coney Island Shop, Mike Hanna; on the B9 bus line in Brooklyn, Hugh Henry; in the Command Center, Anthony Pomilio; in the Times Square subway station, Andy Sparberg; at the Power Control Center, Robert W. Lobenstein and Ed Mallon; and William Tyack and Peter Van Dyk, transit police officers of District One at the Fifty-ninth Street/Columbus Circle Station.

My questions about the world of transit work were generously answered by Charles Seaton of MTA New York City Transit; Al O'Leary, Director of Employee Communication and formerly of the New York City Transit Police Department; Robert Wechsler of the education office of the Transport Workers Union; Bill Murphy of *Newsday,* and Professor Joshua B. Freeman of the Queens College History Department. I thank them all.

A draft of *Transit Talk* was read by a group of readers assembled by the Transit Museum whose suggestions and criticisms improved this book. I thank Joshua B. Freeman, Kathleen Condon, Ellen McHale, Sally Yerkovich, Steve Zeitlin, and Mary A. Zwolinski.

For the sake of accuracy and consistency, the individuals quoted in *Transit Talk* are identified, unless otherwise noted, according to their job at the time of the interview. Where pseudonyms are used they are identified as such. While every effort has been made to keep the force and flavor of these accounts, a degree of editing has been necessary to clarify and condense unclear or repetitive passages. Following the format of other oral histories, I have used ellipses to indicate significant omissions. Readers desiring to see the unedited transcriptions will find them in the archives of the New York Transit Museum.

Transit Talk is conceived as a book of memory and as a popular history and it stands on the shoulders of previous works that provide more definitive histories of the transit system: Josh Friedman's *In Transit*, Clifton Hood's *722 Miles*, and Brian J. Cudahy's *Under the Sidewalks of New York*. It also owes a debt to Jim Dwyer's *Subway Lives*, a valuable account of life and work in the contemporary transit system.

Steve Rivo helped me with the computer work necessary to turn many pages of interview manuscripts into the beginnings of a book; George Cintron and Wendy Boyd provided helpful computer advice during the completion of the book. Kathleen M. Collins provided helpful research assistance. Alexis Kim offered useful suggestions on the introduction and conclusion. Charles Knittle read the entire manuscript and offered valuable editorial advice.

At Rutgers University Press, Marlie Wasserman gave this project vital encouragement. Stuart Mitchner went beyond the customary duties of copyeditor and helped improve the readability of the manuscript.

My wife, Clara Hemphill, gave me the great benefit of her encouragement and her editorial judgment. My son, Max, was excellent company, at the age of fourteen months, on a research trip to Staten Island conducted by bus. My daughter, Allison, who arrived while I was revising the book, provided enjoyable distractions from my work.

My grandfather, Emil A. Ossmann, was a towerman on the New York City subways. His forty-eight years of work kindled the interest that made me want to tell the stories of New York City transit workers. This book is dedicated to his memory.

TRANSIT TALK

Union Square Station.
PHOTOGRAPH © SYLVIA PLACHY 1998.

INTRODUCTION

> People still catch trains, trains still run on tracks,
> and the main thing is still . . . taking people from
> point A to point B. But it's not as simple as that:
> there's a lot of work that goes into this. A lot of
> work that people don't see: like the towermen in
> the tunnels and whatnot; the planning or the buying
> or the laying of tracks. This is a mega-operation.
>
> *Whitfield Lee*, Railroad Clerk[1]

One of the paradoxes of New York City is that so many
people unknowingly rely on each other for the basics
of everyday existence. The lives and labor of 44,310
transit workers are part of this paradox—transit workers like
those you will meet in these pages who every day transport five
million people.[2] In the process, they shape their own lives and
the life of the city around them.

Transit work can be hard, dirty, tedious, stressful, and dangerous. Critic Paul Fussell once observed that in the simplest
calculation there are only two classes of people: those who might
get hurt or killed on the job and those who won't.[3] Transit
workers, especially those who work on subway tracks, belong
to the class that can get hurt or killed on the job. When they
step onto a track to fix a signal, or go to work inches away from

a third rail sizzling with six hundred volts of electricity, they face danger to make things safer for the rest of us.

They also ease the anonymity of the city. When a bus driver gives directions to a bewildered passenger or a railroad clerk keeps watch over a lonely subway station, New York seems to be a more welcoming place.

For New York's 7.3 million people, the transit system is a common thread: every day, 3.5 million people travel along 656 miles of subway track while 1.5 million travel over 1,745 miles of bus routes.

As Raymond Berger, assistant analyst, car equipment, puts it:

⁞⁞⁞⁞⁞   You can get a bus or a train at any hour of the day or night. We're lucky like that. You can talk about a little spot down at the bottom of Kennedy Airport to all the way down in Tottenville in Staten Island, you can get there at any hour of the day or night. That's a pretty good deal. That's what makes New York vibrant.[4]   ⁞⁞⁞⁞⁞

Buses and subways are fixtures in New York life, but there is an entire world that even the most constant rider cannot know: the world of stories, thoughts, and feelings of the 44,000 workers of MTA/New York City Transit—from the most visible bus driver to the least visible mechanic. In *Transit Talk* that world finds its voice as they describe their work and their lives.

MTA/New York City Transit is a sprawling, bureaucratic, industrial enterprise—the largest transit system in the United States. It is woven into the fabric of the city in ways that shape the everyday lives and perceptions of transit workers.

The system is old. The first subway line, the Interborough Rapid Transit Company (IRT), opened in 1904. The subways are filled with structural idiosyncrasies because they were built piece by piece, largely by competing private companies, and were unified under public ownership only in 1940, after more than thirty years of operation. Bus routes, also operated at first by private companies, have come under public ownership more gradually, with some private lines still in operation. In 1953 the New York State Legislature created The New York City Transit Authority as a public corporation to manage and operate most city bus and subway routes; in 1968, the legislature created the Metropolitan Transportation Authority, which then became the Transit Authority's parent agency.

The age of the system makes it a meeting place for the past and the present: in the subways, automated turnstiles for computerized fare cards stand before intricate mosaics laid down by Italian craftsmen more than ninety years ago. In the older elements of the system—such as subway trains, tracks, and signals—mechanization has not yet taken over completely. Everyday work still demands a high degree of individual skill and responsibility. Whether swinging a sledgehammer in track repair, or operating a train in a long tunnel, transit workers see the immediate results of their labor.

On the job, transit workers learn to be part of a team. Track workers learn to watch out for each other to avoid accidents; train operators and conductors learn to work together to keep a train running; bus drivers learn to share information about traffic conditions. They support each other and their labor supports a metropolis: they knit neighborhoods into a functioning city.

The vast scale of MTA/New York City Transit can also create some very human nooks. Holding down a specific job in a large organization can lead a worker to identify with his or her own corner of the larger system. Transit workers fill out the contours and history of such corners with the stories related here. Their stories tell you about how work gives them an identity: the satisfaction that comes from fixing a damaged subway car, the wisdom that comes from mastering a dangerous workplace, the emotional wounds that come from tending to someone injured in an accident, the frustration that comes from difficulties with management, and the happiness that comes from looking back at a productive career. They tell how years spent in the same shop create bonds between workers. They talk of the hurt that comes from laboring in a twenty-four-hour system with night shifts and weekend workdays that take them away from families and loved ones. The transit workers' pride is a bittersweet pride.

Transit workers are part of the solid wage-earning, tax-paying

core of the city's economy. This is as true for the newest members of the transit labor force as for the oldest: African Americans and Latinos, like their Irish and Italian predecessors, have
found steady work in transit. In a city where many manufac-
turing jobs have disappeared, along with the prospects of modest prosperity for working New Yorkers, transit is one place
where you can still make a decent living with your hands.
Moreover, in a city where many hard-working and productive
citizens have fled to the suburbs, the transit workers who have
remained give strength and stability to the neighborhoods where
they work and live.[5]

The workers you will meet in this book are mostly people
with many years, even decades, on the job. Many of them
learned their trade from the first generation of modern transit
workers—the people who worked on the IRT. Now, as they
approach retirement, they run a transit system that is adopting
twenty-first-century technology. In between, they have seen
major changes: the municipal takeover of the subways, union-
ization, racial integration, changing roles for women transit
workers, and the rise of a service economy ethos for transit in
which the people who ride on trains and buses are conceived
of more as customers than as passengers. Through it all, however, transit workers are industrial workers. They submit their
bodies and brains to the ceaseless pressures of a vast bureau-
cracy, teeming crowds, and steel wheels that roll down subway
tracks with overwhelming power.

When transit workers tell stories about their time on the job,
they interpret their experiences and turn them into a kind of
poetry. They become the artists of their own lives.

The stories collected in this book are woven into two strands:
from the beginning of a working life to the end of a working
life and from the most visible segments of the transit system to
the least visible. The chapters go from job-hunting to retirement and from running subway stations to running repair yards,
with pauses along the way to explore stories about race, unions,
and the relations between men and women in the transit
workforce.

The memories recorded here are, unavoidably, subjective:

there are probably as many ways of making sense of transit work as there are transit workers. About one hundred transit workers were interviewed in the making of this book, and a different one hundred might have painted a different picture. Neither picture would be accurate or inaccurate, just more or less faithful to the myriad human experiences that are part of transit work in New York City.

CHAPTER 1

WAR STORIES

If it happens, it happens in the subway.

Lionel Bostick, Assistant Station Supervisor[1]

Transit workers have a name for their greatest tales: war stories. When they tell these stories, they find meanings in their jobs that transcend civil service titles or job descriptions, becoming the stars of their own comedies and tragedies as they present their particular vision of the most profound and universal human experiences, from birth to rescue to death.

Joe Caracciolo, a maintenance supervisor, was riding a train to check on his men when the train unexpectedly stopped on the Broad Channel Bridge. He and the motorman walked to the last car to investigate the trouble. On the way they passed a woman and two teenage girls. The woman said: "Oh my God, somebody help me. Oh my God, somebody help me."

> I just turned around, I said, "What's the problem?"
> So one of the girls said, "She's having a baby."
> That's when *I* said, "Oh my God!"

So I went over, to just talk to her, be nice to her, make her feel all right. And what had happened was she had just started getting severe pains. I had one of the girls time the pains, the other girl wiping her forehead with a handkerchief, and we started doing Lamaze method. . . . And after that—she wouldn't lay down, she was just breathing with me. She started punching me because the pains were getting severe.

I started joking around with her. I said, "What are you hitting me for? I didn't have nothing to do with it. Hit your husband—he's the one that did this to you. I wasn't even there to watch."

So after a while I said, "Come on, lay down, get comfortable." She wouldn't lay down, she wouldn't do any of this.

All of a sudden she said, "It's time. The baby's coming. I got to lay down." It's the truth.

So she lays down on the seat . . . pulled her pants down, the bag came out, the baby's head came out, and the baby flew out. It landed right in my shirt. That's how the baby was born.

Then I lay the baby on top of the mother, make a little joke, "Congratulations, you've got a beautiful baby boy." I says, "Name him Charles from the C Train."

She says, "No, what's *your* name?"

I says, "Joe."

She says, "My son's name is Joseph."

And we couldn't get the baby to cry. So after it took a while for the baby to cry, then it started turning blue on us, and I turned around to the conductor, I said, "I don't care how you do it, or what you do, you've got to get this train to the station, the baby's here. And I want police and paramedics there."

And they uncoupled another car, they pushed us into the station, they had the cops and the paramedics waiting for us when the doors opened up, they came in and they cut the cord, and they started breathing down the baby's mouth with a tube and everything turned out all right. Everybody worked. It was unbelievable. It was like little Joe's lucky day—everybody did something to bring that baby into the world.

I just happened to be there at the right place at the right time. But as far as I'm concerned, everybody—the two teenage girls, there was a Jamaican woman that came out of nowhere, there was the cops, the paramedics, the motorman who got the train going back in, the conductor—everybody just worked together. It was really nice. But when that baby was born and he started crying and everybody started hugging and kissing everybody—it was the greatest feeling in the world. I mean after it was all over, it was, like, unbelievable. For ten, fifteen minutes, I was on the train with the United Nations! And everybody's friend! And everybody was hugging and kissing everybody, it was unbelievable. Then it was all over, and I wanted to kidnap the baby back to New York.

Then I called up 116th Street, I called up the office to tell them where I was and what had happened, and nobody believed me, and I said, "I'm serious!" and they finally started believing me. Then I turned around, and the baby was gone, the mother was gone, they took them all to the hospital. . . . There were so many people that helped out, but according to the mother and the husband, I was the next best thing since sliced bread. . .

To this day, she says I was the only one that made her comfortable.[2] ⫼

Roland E. Shelton Sr. was working a midnight tour as a train master at Grand Central when he received a call that a man was down underneath a train at 137th Street on the Number 1 Line. He went to 137th Street, and was asked to go to the man's house and tell his kin, including his eighty-seven-year-old mother, that he was dead. It was two in the morning. He went with another man and a police officer.

⫼   And that was the hardest thing that I have ever

done in my life, and it's the worst feeling that I have
ever had, because you're there, you're helpless, you
can't do anything. The family is crying. You're trying
to help them out as much as you can. There's nothing
you can do. That was one of the things as a train master
that I hope that I'd never do again. In life, not as a train
master, but in life at all. I found that very hard.[3] ‖‖‖

If it is hard to explain a death to a stranger, it can also be hard
for a transit worker to explain death to the people closest to
him. Like police officers and fire fighters, transit workers sometimes learn to bury their deepest emotions to spare loved ones
from stories of death and maiming on the job. Director of
Emergency Response Jeffrey Van Clief once took his wife to a
doctor's appointment at Eighty-sixth Street and Park Avenue.
On the way home, a young woman jumped in front of the
train. Her legs were cut off. Van Clief told his wife to go up to
the mezzanine of the station while he tended to business.

‖‖‖   I had to check the train, help take her out. Unfortunately she passed away on the way to the hospital.
Made sure no damage was done to the train. . . .
Sometimes a body can do a lot of damage to a train. It
will rip your pipes out, rip your wires down. . . .
I got everybody's name, I got her age, where she
lived at, the cop on the scene, the motorman, the
conductor, emergency medical people, what hospital
she was going to. It's a big process you're going
through. Then you check the car and make sure that
everything is okay . . . and then you call all this in. Like
I say, I was on my way home when this thing happened. I went upstairs, told my wife to give me a
towelette, cleaned my hands up.
I went home and I sit down and I eat. And my wife
is staring at me. I say, "What's the matter?"
She says, "How can you sit there and eat?"
I say, "Why, what's the matter?"
She says, "I don't know if you realize what
happened."

"What do you mean? What happened?"

She says, "A woman got run over, got her legs taken off and you're under the car with her and helping everybody down in the car and you come home and you eat a big meal like that."

She says, "I think about it and I can't even eat."

I say, "I'm hungry."

She says, "Well, is this what you feel?"

I say, "No, this is part of the job. The first time that this happened if you can remember it was a man that got electrocuted and how I felt when I came home. I felt terrible when I came home."

Second time I felt a little bit bad but not as worse as the first time. As it went on I got used to it. If you're in the scene, if you're in the area, then it becomes an everyday job. It's part of this job. If you can't take this type of work, leave it.

The only one that affected me was I had a little boy about twelve years old fall between the cars and take his leg off. That bothered me because I felt that that could have been one of my grandchildren.[4] ▥

Out of attempts to make sense of death can come the knowledge that makes for safety. Paul Prinzivalli, an instructor in safety and general track duties, uses the story of an accident to remind his workers of the need for constant caution around the trains. Once, he relates, he saw a man rushing for one train bump a man into the path of another train.

▥ As he nudged him, the train came, he nudged him far enough for the side of the train to hit his head. Boom! It hit his head, he cracked it, blood splattered. He [the man who nudged him] made the local just before the doors closed up, he worked his way in, it pulled out. He didn't even realize he'd killed a man. That man was a DOA. On the platform dead.[5] ▥

Some of the most memorable stories that transit workers tell are about lives saved—a reminder of the interdependence of total strangers that makes city life civilized. Joseph Tesoriero, a maintenance supervisor, recalls that once he was replacing wooden flooring at a station in Brownsville, Brooklyn, near the end of the New Lots Avenue line, when a train pulled in. At that point on the line, the last car is usually empty, but there were two passengers in the last car: a seated woman and a man standing in front of her. A mugging was in progress.

‖‖‖ Out of the corner of her eye she spotted us, and she started yelling for help. Just as that happened, the doors of the train were closing. We tried to hold the doors—you know, you can't pull the doors back, you can only pull them back so far—and I'm screaming to the conductor, "Open the doors!"

So this fella that was in the car, he didn't know who we were, whether we were the police, so he just stood, he froze. Because she already had her pocketbook out, and you could see her wallet was open. She was reaching in when she saw us. So she got up, we [got in and] finally grabbed him. We squeezed her out between the doors. And this poor woman, she was scared to death. She was hugging the three of us, like we knew her for life. She was petrified. She told us she was a social worker and she was going to visit somebody. We brought her downstairs, we hailed a cab, and we sent her back to Manhattan.[6] ‖‖‖

Paul Prinzivalli tells of a rescue, performed one night after work, when he convinced a troubled woman that she was not alone in the world.

‖‖‖ I left my office at twelve o'clock midnight. I was on the four-to-twelve shift that time. And I always ride the head car going toward South Ferry because I live in Staten Island. So I'm right in the head car, and we're coming into Franklin Street and I see a shadow leaving the platform limits, like looking out.

Well, sometimes people do that, and sometimes

jumpers do that, you know? All of a sudden, we're only maybe about a hundred feet from the station platform, she just jumps right out in front of us. A woman jumped right in front of us—and I'm there, because I could see it point blank—[the operator] dumped the train [applied the emergency brake]. . . . He was very fast, thank God.

And I'm listening, and I don't hear no noise. See, if the train goes over any objects that are sitting on the rail, you'll hear a little "thp"—like a thump, the vibrations come though—I don't hear nothing, I says, "Thank God."

So now we're in the station about over three and a half car lengths, so I knocked at the [operator's] door real heavy. . . . So I identify myself: "Look, I'm a foreman, stay calm, secure your train." Meaning that he's got to put the hand brakes on. I know he's going to be there a while. I ran over and pulled the emergency alarm. When I did that, I got on the phone, called up and said, "This is Prinzivalli on my way home. We have a person under the train. I don't know if she's living, I don't know if she's dead. Get emergency here right away. And I'll take care of matters until they come." I told the Command Center that. . . .

So, I asked the train operator again, "Control yourself." The train is secured—and I told the Command Center, "Keep the power off on the southbound local and southbound express," because you see when they jump, they keep crawling, if they don't get killed, and touch the third rail. . . .

So I ended up crawling—in my dress clothes, I'll never forget it—I banged my head, I've got blood coming down, crawling underneath, and finally I see this lady, well-dressed, laying in the trough. Now the trough is a drainage area of a type-2 track. She's laying in the middle of the trough, her eyes closed.

So I went, "Madam, open your eyes please."

She opened her eyes. . . .

I says, "Madam, do you understand me? Nod your head."

What I was doing there is to find out if there's any spinal problems. So she nodded her head. Thank God, that means no damage to the neck.

I says, "Can you move your right hand?" She moved it. "Move your left hand." Moved it.

"Can you raise your right knee?" She raised her right knee. "Raise your left knee."

"Ahh," I said to myself, "this is a miracle." She landed but didn't get hurt. She got a little dirty and all that. I says, "How do you feel?"

She says, "Oh, I wish I was dead."

I says, "Why did you do this?"

She says, "No one loves me."

I says, "I love you. Why would I crawl under all these cars? I tell you what: remain where you are. If you have any ideas, discard them from your mind. I'm going to have you removed and you're going to be all right. It was God's fate that you shouldn't go this way. Don't worry."

So I came back to the station, crawling underneath, I ripped my pants, the train operator told me, "Hey, you got blood."

I said, "Don't worry about the blood." I look around and the train operator is still a little nervous, and I see the transit cop, a newly appointed transit cop, nice brand-new uniform. I says, "Officer, see the pocketbook laying up against the wall? All right. Train operator, make sure nobody touches that pocketbook. And make sure nobody gets out of the cars. Just tell the passengers to stay calm and everything will be straightened out." There weren't too many people in the train at that hour.

So I looked at the cop, I says, "Officer, come on down here. Assist me to remove a live human being from the tracks."

"Who? Me?"

"Officer, I'm not asking you, I'm telling you: get down here. Give your hat to the train operator and come down here."

So we crawled under . . . and we got in there. I says, "She's OK. You know what we're going to do? You get her under the arms, and I'll get her by the legs, and nice and easy, we'll put her on the ties and then over the rail and then we'll just go along nice and easy, crawling." Three car lengths we were—till we get to the station limits, and then with the assistance of the train operator we get her on the platform, nice and safe, before the ambulance crew came. That's how fast I worked it.

So we got her on the platform, and when the ambulance crew came, I informed them that . . . she did not faint. See, sometimes, people faint and then they misjudge it as a jump. She actually observed the train coming and jumped. "I saw her. I'm a witness, take my name, because she needs medical attention. She needs a lot of help because she's very depressed and she'll do it again if you let her out." I had heard stories about where people were removed from the track and then discharged from the hospital and then two hours later we found out the same party committed suicide, that nobody gave a truthful report on the condition. . . .

So it ended up I gave the train master a full report, everything's back to normal, and I'd missed my boat. I felt raggedy, like I was a homeless person. I was full of grease, my face—I didn't realize how dirty I was because there were no mirrors, you know. My God, when I got home, my face, I had grease here, grease underneath my arm, my pants were ripped, good gabardine.

My wife said, "What happened?" Because she used to wait up for me when I come home, she was worried: she thought something happened. I didn't get home until after 3:30 in the morning. So I told her the story,

we had coffee, I calmed down—I started cooling down
a little bit. . . . The next day I didn't say nothing about
it. . . . Several months went by, and I happened to meet
the train master that I dealt with that particular tour. He
said, "You, you did a great thing. You got a commendation, didn't you?"

I said, "No, I didn't get no commendation."

"That was beyond the scope of duty. You could
have ignored it. You were going home."

"Listen, I don't know about a commendation. I
didn't get one."

"Well," he says, "you know, I got a report that the
transit cop got a day off with pay and a citation for
being a hero."

"Wait a minute, wait a minute, wait a minute. What
did the transit patrolman say?"

He said, "Well, he was the one that got assistance
and removed the person."

"Well, that's nice," I says. "That's a good morale
builder for the transit police. I'm not against that. But to
be honest with you, I ordered him to come down and
assist me. I'm Supervision, not him.

So, it's OK. Another couple weeks went by, and I
got a commendation, beautiful write-up—with the
truth in it. ⁞⁞⁞⁞

CHAPTER 2

GETTING ON BOARD

I never regretted a day that I worked in the Transit
Authority. Because before I got this job I worked
in the garment district seventeen years, and when
I got my first paycheck—I was making thirty-six
dollars a week in the garment district—it was
eighty-four dollars. And I made a vow that I would
always do as good a job as possible.

Joseph Allotta, Cleaner[1]

J ob hunters in Transit have a destination: steady work.
From the Irish immigrants of the 1920s to the Jamaican
immigrants of the 1990s, the first attraction of Transit is
that it provides a regular paycheck. Workplace bonds and friendships, fulfillment and professional advancement—if they do arrive—come later. Officer John Maye, who found a career
policing the transit system, says,

IIIIII   I was born in the Bronx, went to school in the
Bronx, was raised in the Bronx, and still live in the
Bronx. My father was in construction years ago, and

during the Depression most of the people who were
working were civil servants. So for years we'd heard
from him, if you're going to make a career out of
anything, make a career out of the civil service, because
in the worst times, they always have food on the
table.[2] ‖‖‖

Richie Triolo of the lighting department has his own phrase
for it. "I refer to it as 'secure poverty.' You'll never be a mil-
lionaire but you'll always survive and have money to eat and
pay the rent. So I'm still here." Victor De Santo, a line supervisor, echoes his sentiment: "You never get rich but you never
starve."[3]

For African Americans, who struggled in the 1930s and 1940s
to overcome discriminatory hiring practices, and who still face
that discrimination in many fields, transit jobs can be highly
valued. In the 1950s, Whitfield Lee was one of the first to learn
their worth.

‖‖‖   I was born in South Carolina. My family moved to
Brooklyn, New York, in 1937. My father came here
to find a job. At that particular time, it was impossible to
find a job in South Carolina. Everybody was very poor.

I remember coming to New York. We had one bed
and milk crates to sit on. We lived on Lexington
Avenue in Brooklyn, between Nostrand and Marcy.
The old Lexington Avenue El, BMT El, used to run
down Lexington Avenue. In the summer, we used to
sleep out on the fire escape, and when the trains come
by, you waved to the people on the trains. . . .

I wanted to be an artist, but due to other circumstances, I never followed my dream. As boys get older,
they have to have their own money, so I dropped out
of school and went to work. My first job was at a
factory where they make leather watch straps. . . .

One day my youngest brother, Jackie, said, "Let's
take a Civil Service test."

I said, "Aaah, I don't want to be bothered."

He said, "Come on."

So we went down and we took the test and Transit called me and Housing called him. We took the test in 1955, and we both were called in 1957. I was a Railroad Porter. . . .

Let me explain to you: when you know yourself that you don't have that much education or that much qualifications, and you've been working the factories, when you get a job like Transit, I was proud. I used to wear my uniform and cap in the street. . . . Course, some of the guys on the block that I grew up with, they went the other way. When you got a job with Transit or the Post Office, that was quite an achievement. As a matter of fact, I think my first check with Transit was eighty dollars. And that was big money to me then— eighty dollars, wow! I was a porter for eight and a half years.[4] ||||||||

Women are more recent arrivals in Transit. Since the 1970s, urged on by economic necessity and the rise of feminism, women have been entering a variety of transit positions. Chief Station Officer Carol Meltzer graduated from college in 1973 with a major in political science and a minor in economics. She looked at a wide range of city government agencies. Again   and again they turned her down, citing her lack of business experience.

|||||||| When I got to the Transit Authority I was getting desperate. And I really needed money, I mean, I was dead broke. And I needed a job pretty bad.

Now, again, Transit was interesting to me anyway. I got into the room and I started talking and I started to get the, "No, we need somebody with a business degree." Except something interesting happened. At the interview, two gentlemen were conducting the interview. . . . This was back in 1973, I think, prior to women's rights really getting hot and heavy.

And the two gentlemen said something to the effect of, "You know, there aren't very many women managers in Transit."

And all of a sudden I realized that I might have hit onto something here. It was a good opportunity to get myself the job. And I said, "Well, why the hell not?" I said, "Well, how many have you hired today?"

And they looked at each other and all of a sudden the conversation stopped and they said, "Could you excuse us for one minute?"

I said, "Certainly." And they stopped and they came back and they had a whole 'nother attitude. . . . And all of a sudden the questions became a lot more positive and I was offered the job at the end.[5] IIIIII

Meltzer, like many women who have no close friends or relatives in Transit, had to find her own way into the system. Many men, on the other hand, have benefited from the guidance or encouragement of fathers, uncles, brothers, and friends who work in Transit. When he was a child, Don Harold, who worked for the Transit Authority in community relations and public affairs, learned about the system from his grandfather.

IIIIII   My grandfather was with the old Brooklyn Rapid Transit since shortly after the turn of the century. He had been an inspector on the trolleys for many years and then during the Depression they drastically reduced the number of inspectors and he was put back to being a motorman, and he only worked another five years and then retired and passed away. . . .

But he used to take me on rides on his day off. And he rode me throughout the entire system, taught me the lines, taught me the system, told me the background of the system—for instance he would point out, "Well, this car used to be one of the old Coney Island and Brooklyn cars," and then he would tell me what lines the Coney Island and Brooklyn ran before they became part of the Brooklyn Rapid Transit system, and then how the BRT became the BMT, and he filled me in on all that sort of thing. And he would teach me the lines. . . . And if I didn't remember he'd get annoyed, so I had to remember. He did a pretty good job of teaching me. . . .

My grandfather taught me the basics. He never had me run a car, but he taught me all the fundamentals. One of his friends put me to the test when I was about thirteen one time and found out that I had learned rather well, and after that I did quite a bit of rather surreptitious operating in the Brooklyn System and did it until the lines ended.[6] ⅏

An office associate in labor relations for the Transity Authority born and raised in Brooklyn, Mildred Hunter came from a family of transit workers. The first was her uncle, Ira Hughes. Then came her Aunt Celie—raised in Toomsboro, Georgia—who came to New York after a stint driving a taxi in Detroit. During World War II, when women were hired to replace the men who were away in the armed forces, she remembers that Aunt Celie became the first African American woman to drive a bus in New York City.

⅏ Me and my friends used to come down to the Williamsburg Bank and we would meet her and we would put our nickel in the turnstile—at that time the buses had turnstiles—and she would drive us across the Manhattan Bridge into Chinatown. And then she would leave us, and she would tell us what time, the hour, she would pick us back up to bring us back across the bridge. Which was really enjoyable and I felt so proud because she was my aunt driving this bus.

She was a person of determination. . . . And whatever she did, she tried to do it the best she could. Where some people would say, "I can't do this" or "I can't do that," she would say, "You don't know unless you try."[7] ⅏

Chief of Service Delivery Mike Lombardi, an assistant chief mechanical officer at the time of the interview, is the son of a transit worker. He started looking for work after community college.

⫿⫿⫿ I was bumping into guys in the personnel offices of very big companies, and they were tool-and-die makers who had been in the business for thirty years, and they were looking for work. And I was going to compete against these guys. They were much older than I was, of course, and they were saying to me, "Kid, you have a chance, you're starting out. Don't get stuck in this business. You could be a very, very highly skilled tool-and-die maker and every year you're going to be looking for work and worrying about government contracts. You're going to have to relocate all the time."

So it just so happened that I took the test for helper prior to going into college. And just when I got this urge to go travel, they called me off this list. So I thought, heaven, it was my means to go to Europe. . . . I took the vacation time, and came back to the Transit Authority. I went to Europe again during my vacation period. And then there were the promotional opportunities, the civil service. You couldn't be discriminated against, because it was a civil service job. No one really cared what your nationality or race was or what schools you had gone to or what social standard you were. If you could get the mark on the test, you got the job. That's pretty comforting in this world where people tend to get jobs because of who they know.[8] ⫿⫿⫿

Joe Caracciolo was less interested in work and more interested in having a good time. But his father wanted him to get a job.

⫿⫿⫿ I was never really interested in it. And what happened was, I came out of the Navy. And after I came out of the Navy, I didn't want to do anything. I wanted to play beach boy. So my father went down for the application and handed it to me, and he says, "Fill it out." So I filled it out, I sent it in, so the application came for the test. My father handed it to me and says,

"Here, go take the test. You don't take the test, don't come home."

I went on the trains . . . the two trains came in at the same time, and I says, "If I go that way, I've got to go take the test; if I go that way, I go to the beach, have a great time at the beach. If I go that way to the beach, I go home, my father's going to kill me." I says, "I'll go that way and take the test!" And that's how the saga goes, how I got the job at the Transit Authority.[9] ⅠⅠⅠⅠⅠ

The first step in getting a job as a blue-collar worker in Transit is to take a civil service test for an individual job—bus driver, for example. Then, depending on how well you do on the test, you choose your work assignment—its tours, hours, and route— at a "pick." Picks are held periodically and are open to virtually all transit workers. Applicants who do best on the appropriate civil service test, and who have seniority, get first choice in the pick. New transit workers enter the system at the pick; veterans use it to change jobs within the system.

Once hired, a transit worker enters a vast enterprise. For New Yorkers who have lived much of their lives within the confines of their neighborhoods a transit job can take them far from home and out into the wider city for the first time. "My first day on the job," recalls Joseph Tesoriero, "being born and raised in Brooklyn, and not knowing anything past the Brooklyn Bridge, they sent me up to Unionport Road in the Bronx. I thought I needed a passport."[10]

First days on the job can be memorably hard. Brenda Hayes was assigned to a token booth in the Bronx on Tremont Avenue. Soon she was in a mess of tokens, bills, and change.

ⅠⅠⅠⅠⅠ And I'll always remember the young man who now drives a train. And he came in one day and he says, "What are you doing?" And I had money all over the place, on the floor, on the board, and it was time for me to go home and him to come in and I did not know what I was doing. Within thirty minutes he had me completely straightened out. I'll never forget it.[11] ⅠⅠⅠⅠⅠ

The first day on the job means not only learning new work routines, but confronting the gap between the hope for a fulfilling career and the reality of a boring job. At first, Mike Lombardi found it difficult to do the work assigned to him.

ⅢⅢ I went to a four-year technical high school in machine design where we worked eight, nine hours a day in the schoolroom. And we thought we were red hot when we came out of there. A little bit of college. And for the first six months in the Transit Authority my job was to unload and load trucks with heavy equipment. And it didn't look like there was going to be anything beyond that. I was ready to run the place, and here I am unloading trucks. I know you have to start at the bottom. It was very discouraging to think that here we were trained in a technical field, and I'm just loading and unloading trucks. I thought it was very demeaning.

I told my father this at the dinner table, "I'm going to quit this job." That was our usual conversation at night twenty-seven years ago. I was going to quit this place, and he kept saying, "What's wrong?"

"I'm loading and unloading trucks."

And he says, "What kinds of things are you loading and unloading?"

And I say, "Well, you know, I'm unloading brake valves and I'm unloading shoe beams, and I'm unloading things that look like this and things that look like that."

So he says to me, "Well, listen, here's what you gotta do: If you want to get off that job, I'll give you a suggestion. You take everything that you're going to load on to this truck or unload and find out the name of it—of the part, because they're all subway car parts. Find out the name of these parts, find out where they're located on the subway car, and approximately what their function is. What do they do on the subway. What's the purpose of this part. When you think you

can identify all these things and know what they do . . .
go to your foreman and tell your foreman that you
know all about this stuff. And tell him that you're sick
and tired of unloading and loading trucks, and that
you're a pretty bright guy, and I want to do something
else."

So I did that. And the foreman said to me, "That's
really amazing." He said, "That really is. For a young
kid, that's OK." And he said, "I'm going to give you a
different job." So he did give me a different job, a more
interesting job. ⅠⅠⅠⅠⅠ

George Havriliak, a retired mechanical engineer, had to make
a social adjustment.

ⅠⅠⅠⅠⅠ Yes, the first day on the job was cultural shock.
When I went up to East 180th Street, Reggie Welsh
told me that I would be working with a man by the
name of Doug Tilton. And that they had a coffee club
up there. And so, I got on my gray flannel suit, my
white shirt, my black tie with a little yellow stripe in it,
and I packed my work clothes in a gym bag. And
because of the coffee club, my wife gave me a cup and
saucer with gold trim. And I put that in my gym bag
along with my dirty clothes, old clothes, and I went up
to East 180th Street.

I had never been up in that section of the Bronx near
the Bronx Park. And when I walked in, I finally found
Doug Tilton and the crew . . . and they were in a room
with a big table, and they were mostly Irish. And they
were brawny guys, and next to that room was a toilet,
and they had the door open. And on a shelf was a hot
plate and they were boiling some coffee.

And when I looked at these guys, I almost died. Here
I am in my gray flannel suit, and here they are with,
like, cigars out of their mouth[s], disheveled and rough-
looking people. And one guy, Jimmy McHugh—I
remember his name because it was like the song composer—he said, "Hey kid, you take the locker right by

the door, because most people don't stay here very long, and so this way you can leave quickly."

And when I saw these guys drinking the coffee, they said, "Do you have a cup?" and it was the first time I really did some quick thinking. I said, "No, I didn't bring up a cup," because I had a cup and a saucer, gold trim.

And Jim said, "That's OK, we'll give you a cup." And they gave me a cup and it was pretty dirty, and he said, "Don't worry about the dirt, because on Fridays we sanitize all the cups."

And I didn't know what he meant, but I washed out the cup anyway, sat down, had some coffee, and on Friday, he said, "Kid, give me fifty cents."

And I said, "What's the fifty cents for?"

He says, "Well, we buy a bottle of Four Roses and we clean out the cups." He said, "We sanitize the cups."

So there, about three o'clock, out came a bottle of Four Roses, and he pours this straight whiskey into each cup—no ice, no chaser, this is 1958—and they drank straight whiskey right out of the cups. And he says, "Here, now, you see, they're all nice and sanitized; they're nice and clean for Monday morning." And that was the first time I ever nursed a drink in my whole life, because I wasn't really interested.[12]　⦀

For bus driver Dick Hinton [a pseudonym], a job was a way to earn dignity.

⦀　You know, I always had low self-esteem. . . . So when I passed and got the job I felt a lot better about myself. Because I had never been in the service and I had two brothers that [had been] and it was like a comparison game. "Look at your brothers, they made men of themselves." I always felt like I was missing something. So when I became a driver I felt like I was just as good as the next guy.[13]　⦀

CHAPTER 3

STATIONS AND FARES

> After you're down here for a while, I guess you
> could write a book.
>
> *Whitfield Lee*, Railroad Clerk[1]

Dollars and quarters; fare cards and tokens and student passes; hectic crowds and numbing boredom; the chance of a robbery; passengers who hate you and passengers who love you—all of it experienced from inside a tiny soundproof booth. Welcome to the world of the railroad clerk.

The first face of MTA/New York City Transit that subway riders meet is that of the railroad clerk. The job requires mathematical skill, patience, and tact. For passengers, especially late at night, railroad clerks—whose title will change to "station agent" when the introduction of the MetroCard is completed—provide reassuring eyes and ears that reduce the loneliness of a subway platform.

Railroad Clerk Whitfield Lee recalls his routine: arrive on the job, get a pail and "pull the wheels" of the turnstiles (meaning empty them of their tokens), set up his tokens on the left side of his counter, lay out the paperwork he will have to do as he sells tokens—daily report books, remittance slips, and more.

But perhaps the hardest part is the hours. The shifts that people work in a twenty-four-hour transit system can be hard on marriages and personal lives. According to Whitfield Lee,

> ⅢⅢ You have to pay your dues. Tuesday, Wednesday used to be my Saturday, Sunday for a long time. One thing about a job like this, although the new management is a little better on giving people weekends off earlier, is that it has ruined a lot of marriages. This job, post office, and police. Like, you're off Tuesday and Wednesday, maybe you're working nights and your wife's working days, and you're coming and going. You don't see each other at night. ⅢⅢ

To fight the loneliness, railroad clerks often do little things to make a booth feel more like a home. Lionel Bostick put orange peels on the radiator that would give off a nice odor. He brought in a cushion to sit on. Whitfield Lee brought in a radio to keep informed. Other clerks put up holiday greetings.

The need to establish a minimum level of comfort in the booth becomes obvious once you consider all that a railroad clerk does in the course of a day. Working with station managers and cleaning personnel, the clerks try to keep the station orderly despite beggars and fare beaters.

Jeffrey Van Clief, with more than thirty years in Transit, likes to think he can distinguish disabled beggars from scam artists.

> ⅢⅢ There was a guy, he was good, this man was beautiful. He had me fooled. He had no pupils. He had just plain white eyes. There was no color in his eyes, just white. And he used to come on with a cane, and I was at West Fourth Street and he would have another guy leading him around and for years, man, this guy was great.
>
> I felt sorry for him. One night they had asked me to

work overtime until about two o'clock in the morning. . . . So anyhow, I get downstairs and I hear noise under the staircase and I look and there's these two guys. And the guy that's supposed to be blind with the cane is counting money. He was telling the guy, this is for the rent, this is for the food. . . .

As I come around and look, the guy's got eyes. You know what this guy was doing? I found out later on. I become friendly with the guy that's leading him around. He says, "Oh, that's easy, man. They break an egg and you know the white membrane you pull off? They pushed that white membrane in his eye. And it discolors your eye." And this guy was leading him around. So the scams have been here, they've always been here.[2] ⅢⅢ

Fare beaters, on the other hand, use mechanical strategies, as Carol Meltzer observes.

ⅢⅢ A new scam came up whereby the vandals would come and . . . make something out of a Coke can or a beer can which looks like a "V" and they would actually stick that into the non-registering fare box and then wait until some tokens accumulated and then just kind of pull it out and here are all these tokens, you know, in this little "V" that they've created. . . . Token suckers [who jam the token slot, then suck out the tokens and use or sell them for their own purposes] are still a problem.[3] ⅢⅢ

Whitfield Lee sees himself as part of the first line of defense. Once a clerk gets a reputation for letting fare beaters through the turnstile, the dam is broken.

ⅢⅢ So you challenge them or just say, "Hey, pay your fare," because some people don't want to be embarrassed. Most of them will run through, but some of them won't . . . 'cause they don't know if a cop's in the station or not. But if you just sit there and don't say nothing, then you're enticing more fare beaters. But

[with kids] you can get a little control over a station.
Especially if you get to know the parents. Once they
know that you know their mothers or their fathers,
that's when you get control. Because I say, "I'll tell
your mother next time."   ⅢⅢ

Clerks learn to cope and shrug off the occasional nasty passenger or the fellow railroad clerk who shows up late to take
over the booth. It is never easy. General Superintendent Brenda
Hayes recalls that her toughest assignment as a railroad clerk
was in a booth at 125th Street and Eighth Avenue, working the
shift from two p.m. to ten p.m. She recalls that "the hardest
part of the job was dealing with the public."

ⅢⅢ   One of the people that picked the job before me
said to me, "How can you pick that job?"
And I'll never forget saying, "How bad could it be?"
I says, "I am going to be in a black neighborhood and I
am a black person. I don't think I can have much of a
problem."
Well, I tell you that was the worst! I have never been
called so many names. The people there, if the tokens
were sixty cents, they just expected you to let them go
through: "I only have thirty-five cents today." They
accused you of being just a slave, you're this, you're
that. I mean, the people were so rude.
I always said that once a person stepped into the
subway that was when their personality changed.
People expected so much. They would bang on the
window. They could not understand that when we
came down to train to be a railroad clerk that the
Transit Authority does not teach you where the Metropolitan Museum of Art is. . . . It's something that a
clerk has to learn on their own. Of course they supply
us with maps and books but we have to take time to
look through that. And people, they did not understand. They wanted their questions answered first. They
wanted their tokens right away. And most of them

wanted one or two tokens and were always giving you large bills.[4] ⅢⅢ

For years, the worst hazard of the clerk's job was the hold-ups. Token booths used to be wooden structures with metal bars on the windows, but a wave of robberies in the 1970s changed that. At first, criminals pulled guns on clerks or stole tokens from them as they emptied the turnstiles. The Transit Authority responded by installing fortified steel and fiberglass booths. In the late seventies, robbers escalated their tactics and began to set fire to the booths. A clerk would usually run out of the structure and leave the money behind for the taking. In 1979 two clerks were burned to death in an attack. In 1988 a clerk was burned to death in a robbery. The Transit Authority installed fire extinguishers that eventually provided a measure of safety. Nevertheless, in 1989, when Whitfield Lee was interviewed, robberies of railroad clerks were almost a daily event in New York City.[5]

> ⅢⅢ I've been held up five times. One year . . . two guys came into the station and they stood there and they smoked a reefer or two. Before I know they came over to the window and pushed a gun in. Usually the guys didn't come into the booth: they took the money from the window and run. But this time they came in. It's the intimidation. They try to talk to you: "I ought to kill you, I ought to kill you!"
>
> You get scared later. After it's over. You get scared, then you get mad. Because I don't care who it is, nobody likes for anybody to take anything from him. Even though that's Transit's money, they're intimidating YOU or threatening bodily harm to YOU, and you don't even know this person. So you get mad after that.
>
> I never thought about leaving. . . . You could get held up walking the street. This way, you get paid for it. ⅢⅢ

John Waddell, another railroad clerk, agrees about the hazards.

‖‖‖   It's a good job but it's gotten pretty dangerous. In fact, my daughter tried it and she only lasted three months. She was afraid, and I can understand it. I tried to encourage her to stay. And she said, "Well, Daddy, it's different. You're a man." She was afraid. I could understand that.[6] ‖‖‖

Fortunately for the railroad clerks, police have drastically reduced token booth robberies. In general, since 1990, aggressive and innovative policing strategies have cut subway crime overall and token booth robberies in particular. In the late 1970s, ten booths were robbed every week. By 1994, the rate of booth robberies dropped to seven in the first six months of the year.

Still, a subway station at night can inspire fear in transit workers. When Brenda Hayes moved from being a railroad clerk to supervising clerks and cleaners, she took on the potentially dangerous duty of checking station conditions. Once, at Clinton and Washington streets in Brooklyn, she examined the condition of the toilets.

‖‖‖   And there was a man that was following me in the bathroom. And the good part about it is that a male clerk yelled out over the speaker and was coming out of the booth. And that was what saved me.

And that was when I decided I didn't want the job anymore. And my supervisor worked here at Jay Street during the night tour and I came down here to see her at three o'clock in the morning and I was upset and I was crying and I gave her my pass and I said, "It's not worth it." I said, "All I have are my sons and, you know, they only have me and if something happens to me what's going to happen to them?"

And she taught me how to make the job work for me. She said to me, "Is there anyone that says that you have to go check that bathroom by yourself? Is there anyone that said that you have to check that bathroom at three o'clock in the morning?" She told me, do what was safe, do what was right for you, that's how you should do your job.

I started to carry schedules around with me. . . . I would only visit stations, unless an emergency came up, that had cleaners at them. And then I would say to the cleaner, "Let's take a walk." And then he would walk me through all the steps and I would check and see if all the lights were working and all that. ⅢⅢ

Although the worst encounters with passengers make the railroad clerk's job difficult, the best encounters are a clerk's salvation. The clerks, as Carol Meltzer observes, are widely appreciated as a force for neighborhood stability.

ⅢⅢ Where do people run when there's something going on in the street, you know, something serious, a shooting, a stabbing? In the middle of the night usually the only thing open is the token booth. And you find all the time they will run down to the token booth and tell the token clerk because they know that he has got a way of getting the police. They are a very, very important part of communities and most clerks will wind up having relationships with people and we get a lot of pleasant letters from people telling us that we have good employees and telling about things they've lost and how this clerk returned that or gave them back their change the next day when they came to the booth and they had given them too much money the day before. ⅢⅢ

On a dark night or a lonely afternoon, an illuminated token booth offers the prospect of human companionship that can stop a crime or ease loneliness. Says Whitfield Lee,

ⅢⅢ One lady said I should get counselor's pay, because people come by, they tell me their problems. One lady, especially, she came by this week and she was telling me her problems. She started crying, and it looks funny to people coming by, because she's crying. They don't know whether I'm making her cry or not.

That's happened a lot over the years. Because if you're not a person who complains yourself, people tend to think that basically you're happy and you're a

well–adjusted person, they'll tell you their problems.
And I get a lot of that. There's a lot of lonely people
out here, people who'd rather tell it to a stranger or
tell it to me because they know it's not going to go
no further than me because I don't know their
families. ‖‖‖

Lionel Bostick, working at a token booth on the West Side
of Manhattan, became friendly with a neighborhood business-
man.

‖‖‖   I met a guy up around Eighty-sixth Street—he
used to come down for change for his business all the
time. He had a restaurant and bar. And he was a very
nice guy. I remember him because he used to bring me
some of the largest sandwiches I've ever seen, big slices
of rye bread. I remember he came down one New
Year's Eve when I was working, very lonely time, and
he got some change and he asked me if I wanted
something to drink, and I said, "No," and he said,
"Well, let me bring you a little snack, anyhow." And he
brought me a big plate with a big sandwich and potato
salad on it and he brought a pitcher of coffee. Most
people were very nice after awhile.[7] ‖‖‖

While working at the Burke Avenue station in the Bronx,
John Waddell had a conversation with a female passenger who
eventually became his wife.

‖‖‖   One day it was raining very hard. There was water
all over the place. I guess it must have been flooding in
the station. So she said, "You're going to need a boat to
get out of there."
    So that's how we got to talking. I said something
like, "Are you married?"
    She said, "No."
    "Do you think you'd like to go out?"
    She said, "Yes."
    So that's how we got started. ‖‖‖

CHAPTER 4

OPERATING TRAINS

> As a conductor you are literally the ambassador.
> You're the one in uniform. You're the one that
> the public sees. You're the one that they take their
> frustrations out on. . . . Oh, I can't tell you the
> number of times I've been spit at and had cans
> thrown at my head.
>
> *Stanley Stern*, Dispatcher and former Conductor[1]

Subways are run by a team. The train operator controls the speed and braking of the train. The conductor controls the doors and makes announcements to the passengers. And the tower operator, sitting in a small control booth, steers the train by directing it onto the right stretch of track. A conductor's mistake can trap a passenger in the closing doors of a subway; an error by a train operator or tower operator can mean a collision and death. When a strike-breaking train operator with virtually no training lost control of his subway at Malbone Street on the Brooklyn Rapid Transit line in 1918, the train derailed and 102 people died. It was the worst accident in subway history. The name Malbone Street became synonymous with tragedy, and the stop was renamed Empire Boulevard.[2]

The subway track is, to the average person, a confusing and dangerous place. Stand at the front end of a subway train and look down the tunnel before you. To an untrained eye it is a forbidding scene: a ribbon of track that runs off into a dark maze. At intersections, the ribbons of track run together into a tangle of steel. Lights to the side of the track shine red, amber, or green. They mean nothing to you—and everything to the train operator, because they are part of a signal system that directs each train onto the proper track and keeps trains from running into each other.

The train operator, who seems at first glance to be steering the train, actually controls only speed and braking. The train is steered onto the proper track by switches under the control of the tower operator whose tower is actually a room at the end of a subway platform; it is called a tower after the elevated structures built by railroads to oversee the operation.

Each tower operator controls a sector of a few miles of track. Inside the cramped quarters of the tower, the operator sits before an electronic board that lights up to reveal the location of trains within the tower's sector. Below the board is a long row of levers that control the switches embedded in the tracks. When the tower operator moves a lever, the corresponding switch on the track goes into position to direct the train onto the chosen track.

Joe Cassar, B1 tower operator, says that his main function

> ‖‖‖‖   is to observe trains coming through the area and if at any point during the rush hour or during the day if any train has any trouble I either turn the train and discharge them and send them back to the yards. My main concern here is keeping schedules, informing other towers of lateness in the system, of any minor delays or major delays, whichever is the greatest. . . .
>
> Basically a tower operator must be alert at all times, must have his eyes and ears open. Really, he needs about three ears and five arms to work a machine.

Because between making decisions and listening to orders from Command Center on the speakers, operating the machine, keeping schedules, answering phones, it takes a little doing. . . . The towers can make you or break you. If you don't pay attention, if you're a lazy daisy, if you don't watch what you're doing you're going to get yourself in a lot of trouble. You keep your mind on the railroad, you have to concentrate on information which is a very important thing. Information must be passed to different towers. If there's anything going down and you don't pass any information and later on Command Center finds out, then you have a lot of problems on your hands.[3] ⅢⅢ

While the tower operator directs the trains onto the proper tracks, block signals—which were part of the original New York subway system—keep enough space between trains so that they do not overtake one another and crash. The operation of the block signal is simple. Individual blocks of track, each about a train in length, are controlled by a signal light and a stop arm. A train operator arriving at the block looks at the light on the side of the track. If the light is green, the block is all clear and the operator can proceed. If it is yellow, the operator proceeds with caution. But if the light is red, another train ahead is in the block. A T-shaped stop arm about a foot long will pop up next to the track and trip a brake lever on the train—stopping the train and preventing a possible collision. (In cases where modern subway cars are so large and fast that they might not stop fast enough to prevent an accident, reductions in speed and acceleration preserve a margin of safety.) Where two lines of track intersect, the system is slightly more complex: a pair of lights tells the train operator which route to take and whether it is clear ahead.

Joseph P. Fox, a senior railroad signal specialist, explains that the system maintains spacing between trains. It can also stop a train running in violation of safety procedures.

ⅢⅢ The system is probably one of the safest in the world. We transport about three and one-half million

people a day. . . . And you very seldom hear of any
accidents. I know we do have a few. Most of them are
due to human failure, rather than equipment failure. So
the signaling system provides the wherewithal so you
can move large volumes of people very closely together
at a rational speed.[4] ‖‖‖

The mechanics of block signals are complemented by human communications. In the Command Center, located at 370
Jay Street in Brooklyn, dispatchers communicate with train
operators via two-way radios. They also speak to tower operators through loudspeakers and telephones. An electronic map
of the entire system was built, but the fiscal crisis of the 1970s
intervened before it was put it into operation. The result: of all
the lines on the subway, only the Woodlawn line is plugged
into the map. For the rest of the system, the Command Center
relies on voice and telephone communications with tower operators to judge the specific condition of trains.

Workers in the Transit Power Control Center on Fifty-third
Street in Manhattan, which controls the flow of traction power
to the entire subway system, know whether power is flowing
to each section of track at all times. But they do not know the
condition of each train.

Transit officials talk about opening a new Command Center
in the twenty-first century. Their goal is to put the Command
Center and the Power Control Center under one roof in Manhattan, enabling them to monitor the entire system with greater
precision. Until then, they will rely on block signals and people.

Signals are one more example of the interdependence of
the transit system. Tower operators, as Cassar explains, learn to
aid and depend on other tower operators up and down the
line.

‖‖‖   See, we help each other out. That's basically a
cardinal rule here. You help the next tower operator. I
mean, the guy's going under for some apparent reason,
if you can help him out do so, because you never know
when you're going to be in a situation. We look out for
each other, we take care of each other over here. We

have an understanding, so to speak. . . . We need information. You get information, I want you to pass it to me. If I get it, I'll pass it to you. ⅲ

The tower operator is physically isolated. The conductor and the train operator, however, have to work as a team: they not only operate a train together, they have to maintain schedules, meet the demands of supervisors, and cope with passengers. In interviews they recount dealings with passengers that consume as much attention as mechanical tasks. Robert Kolacz, acting assistant chief transportation officer, was once operating a train when someone knocked on the door of his cab.

ⅲ I opened the door like and this man said to me, "I'm sorry." And he closed the door. I couldn't figure why this guy said that, unless he thought he was trying to go through the cars and he went the wrong way. Then he came back again. And now he opened the door and he said the same thing, "I'm sorry." And I said to myself, you know, he was an old fellow, like in his fifties or something. You know the man wasn't just clowning around.

And all of a sudden I heard this woman laughing, I mean hysterical, right outside the cab. So I opened it up to look and he's standing there and he had suitcases and he was sitting in the seat right facing across from the cab. And she was with him and she was some relative of his that met him. And then she asked him the second time why he did what he did, why he came up and knocked on the cab. And he had just come up from the South and he traveled only on buses. And he thought, you know, when he went on a trip on the bus, the bathroom was there. And he thought he was interrupting me because I was sitting in the cab there.[5] ⅲ

Not all encounters are so innocuous. As Stanley Stern points out, preoccupied and thoughtless passengers can frighten transit workers.

ⅲ Passengers take chances and they don't realize how

dangerous it can be. Stepping through a doorway while a train is moving and shaking and rocking, they can very easily slip between the cars and fall down and get themselves killed. Daring the conductors to close the doors on them. Stepping into a car at the very last minute instead of waiting a few minutes for the next train, holding doors and getting dragged.

Sometimes—most of the time I would say—it's not the conductor's fault. He's doing his job, and this idiot stepped in the door at the wrong time, and he's fighting the odds, and he's fighting fate. Someday he's going to get hurt. And they turn right around and blame the conductor, when it was their stupidity to begin with—when it was a simple matter, especially during the rush hour, of standing back and waiting another three or four or five minutes for another train. Or leaving five minutes early. ||||||

Assistant Dispatcher Ed Krieger recalls a narrow escape when he was a conductor.

|||||| I had a bottle thrown at me, by friends of mine when I used to work the M Shuttle out in Ridgewood, Maspeth, Middle Village. And there's a park on the side, and my nephews used to hang out there—you know, all the kids, midnights, I was working midnights. And someone threw a beer bottle, a full bottle of beer, at the bulkhead, and it splattered all over me. . . .

I had glass all over me, and I smelled like a brewery. And it was funny: when I went home the next day, I saw my nephew. And he says, "Oh—that's funny, because one of my friends was throwing stuff at the train." So I explained to him that he could have killed me and he could have killed any other conductor. . . . It is dangerous out there for conductors. You got to feel sorry for them. All of them.[6] ||||||

At the same time, conductors and train operators guard the passengers—not only by operating the trains safely, but by pro-

tecting passengers from crime. Conductor Jim Miles [a pseud-
onym] notes,

> |||||| You can see somebody who is up to no good. You
> can basically see it in their eyes. . . . They'll get on the
> train and the first thing that you'll notice is that they're
> looking all around. It's like they're casing the joint. . . .
> But with these kids, what they do, they walk to one
> end, walk to the other, and then as they're walking
> through you can see them looking at one passenger and
> another. And that's what they call "looking for a vic," a
> victim. And they'll walk through once and they'll walk
> back through again. . . . You can see it in their eyes,
> they are looking. They'll look at me and immediately
> avert their eyes.[7] ||||||

Ed Krieger recalls how, as a conductor, he once risked his
own safety to save a passenger on the J line.

> |||||| Kosciusko Street at one time had a disco there, and
> "undesirable" people. And at 3:20 in the morning, there
> was always this one group of kids, about sixty or
> seventy kids, used to get on and start causing havoc on
> the train. But at Broadway and Myrtle, which is the
> next stop, there was always five or six cops there, to get
> on the train and escort these guys off or whatever.
>   And I always used to pick up this one guy—nice
> guy, and he always talked to me—he got on at 168th
> Street at the time. And he always talked to me, he sat
> right by me, right by the cab. . . .
>   But this one day, I open up the door . . . and all of a
> sudden, sixty, seventy of these guys come running over.
> I mean, I was in that station there, without exaggera-
> tion, for five minutes. Until they all got on. They just
> held the doors. You just sit there, right? And I wasn't
> too worried about it, because like I say, you got six cops
> at Broadway and Myrtle. . . .
>   So after we closed down, I hear this "Aaaaaa"
> screaming and I'm looking out the window and I turn

around, I see the guy's neck and head, and I see a pair
of hands around his neck. They were trying to push
him between the cars. . . . My first reaction was, I
grabbed him by the shirt, picked him up, and I put him
in my cab, told him to stay there. I locked my door,
and at Broadway and Myrtle, I started blowing for a
cop. . . .

All the cops come up. There was about five cops
with guns. So they said, "What happened?" I said,
"They almost killed my passenger." He was bleeding
from the eye, nose, and I said, "Don't worry" (he's
crying and everything). I says, "Just relax." I says,
"Identify the guys." He says, "No." I says, "Identify the
guys. Just pick anybody out."

So my friend Frankie, he's got a big mouth, he's a
motorman . . . he likes to fight, so he had his brake
handle, so he says, "Let's get any one of these guys,"
you know, "we'll start banging heads now."

So the cop says, "Just relax, relax," . . . and the guy
wouldn't press charges. So he [the cop] says, "Well,
what we'll do: we'll take half of them off the train. We
can't take them all."

So I says, "OK, we'll leave them on the train." We
pull out of Broadway and Myrtle, and I says, "I'm going
to get killed. None of the cops will come because they
had too many guys they were going to lock up." . . .

When we pulled into Flushing Avenue, they all got
off. . . . There was about maybe fifty of them out there.
I says, "I'm gonna die now, right?" So I told the guy,
"Just stay in the cab, stay near the cab, because if they
start throwing things, I don't want you to get hurt."
And I just closed the window, and I closed the door,
and while I'm looking through the window, you know,
on the side, they were going like this: "Have a nice
night! Have a nice night!"

But after talking to the guy, the guy was still crying,
he was upset, he had cuts on his face, he didn't want no

medical thing—and when he got off at Broad Street, he thanked me.

And I says, "You're going to be a little late for work." He looks at his watch: his watch is gone, his ring is gone, his necklace is gone. They ripped him off, and he didn't realize it. That's how shook up he was.

Never seen him after that. Probably took a bus, or maybe a cab, I don't know if he quit the job—but I never seen him after that.   ⫶

Not all stories of assault end on such a sad note. Conductor Harry Nugent once saw an assault on his train thwarted by an upset stomach.

⫶   I was working on the midnights and very often on midnights people offer up the food they have in their stomach for all to see. And this fellow was sitting right opposite of my cab and he was with his girlfriend or wife or whatever, and he and I knew he was going to be ill, I could just tell. And I said, "Do me a favor and not sit here because I have to work here and I know you're going to throw up." And his wife immediately endorsed him that this man never throws up. Well, she hardly finished that sentence when the floor was completely littered with his whole meal. You know, and it was really bad. Now I'm stuck.

And so we're going along and I'm trying to, you know, I always feel there's a purpose for things in life. And even in this. And there was a gang. I was coming into a station and I saw this gang. They were giving the change clerk a hard time for one thing. They saw the train. Late at night you have to wait if you miss your train so they all went over the turnstile. I had tried to get out because they were all fare beaters and they looked like trouble anyway.

So I tried to get the doors closed before they got on. Almost made it but one guy got his hand in one door. So we opened up. Well, he started cursing at me,

yelling down the platform . . . and so he, you know,
told me to be fruitful and multiply and so on. So he,
they got on the train, now they're about three cars
back. I saw them charging, they're going to get me,
coming up through this train.

Well the leader came up and is coming at me and he
hit the vomit and he went into this long slide. Well, he
really did me a service because he picked up an awful
lot of it, except his leather jacket resisted it somewhat
but his pants were good. So, he got up, his friends
didn't want to go near him. He didn't know what to
do. He lost interest in me, obviously. . . . So it all
worked out rather well.[8]   ‖‖‖

In their working lives, conductors witness an endless parade
of passing strangers. They learn, over the course of many incidents, that some passengers are not what they seem to be at first
glance. Robert Kolacz recalls an incident when he was a conductor one night about eleven p.m. on the F train.

‖‖‖   There was one lady that used to get on, she was a
nurse, I think she got on around Seventh Avenue in
Brooklyn. And she knew me. People at that time of
night will talk to you just to feel safer I guess. So she
used to get on and say, "Hello" and then sit down and
read her paper. She always stayed in my car.

She was in her seat and a blind person got on the
train. And it was a man; he had a stick. . . . Years ago
blind people always carried that colored cane. And so
he got on the train, and I kept the doors open extra
long and I knew that he wouldn't have any trouble
finding a seat because this lady was the only other
person on the train. So I kept the doors open and then I
looked inside so he could get inside. And he was kind of
fumbling around, and the lady said to him, "Are you all
right? Just sit down. There's a seat right there," you know.

And so, we still had the doors open and he stuck the
cane up, his cane stopped the fan and this black soot come
out of there and it covered everything in the car. . . .

The dirt had accumulated in that fan for so long. And then, it all happened so fast, I don't remember how I looked at him but I looked at that lady and she was like plastered to the back of the seat and then she moved up you could see her silhouette behind her. She was covered from head to toe with this black soot. And you could see the silhouette on the thing there. And she started laughing, I started laughing, and this guy, he was supposedly blind, it was so funny he had to start laughing. He wasn't blind, he was just a panhandler.   ⅢⅢ

Humor can also be an effective means of relating to the public. Harry Nugent, the son of a vaudevillian, turned his conductor's job into a theatrical performance to put his passengers at ease and remind them that boarding a subway does not mean leaving civilization. For Nugent, who went into transit work after his job as an executive assistant to the editor of *Look* magazine disappeared with the publication's demise, the routine began as an exercise in crowd control. Consider these excerpts from his show on November 12, 1990.

ⅢⅢ   Is everyone here? Good. We'll dispense with the formalities and get directly to the point. What you've boarded is the Uptown Number 1 and our destination is 242nd/Van Cortlandt Park. We confine our activities to the West Side of Manhattan and we attempt to serve you with most stops along the way. . . . We're in the Twenty-eighth Street station. This is where the flower district, the fur district, the Fashion Institute, all dance to the tune of Tin Pan Alley. . . . Fifty-ninth Street. Same old crowd. John Jay College, Fordham University, Art Student's League, American Bible Society. Same old hangout, Columbus Circle. Of course, if you don't want to hang out we have A and D trains here, along with the B and C. Fifty-ninth Street, Columbus Circle. Good morning and congratulations. You found the 1 that will get you to Van Cortlandt Park and, well, most stops along the way. Our next stop is Sixty-sixth. Doors are closing and welcome. . . .

We are now approaching the terminal at 242nd Street at Van Cortlandt Park. They say all good things must come to an end. I really don't believe it but it is a good thing we're coming to an end for we're running out of stations. But it isn't the end of good things, for here you'll find Van Cortlandt Park. You'll find Manhattan College. You'll find the gateway to Westchester County. Well, whatever you find, we hope you find your day to be most enjoyable and we'd like to thank you for riding with the New York City Transit Authority and the Number 1 in particular. ||||

Nugent's station-to-station patter has a purpose.

|||| What I was really trying to do is make them feel they haven't left civilization when they came down to the subway. And, you know, that they are not in an alien, hostile environment. . . . And I was also trying to break through the hostility barrier that I believe has grown up over the years between the transit employees and the general public. ||||

Nugent believes that his humor and commentary bring out the best in passengers.

|||| And I watch people when they are treated with compassion and treated with care, interest, just bloom when you deal with them. For instance, I had a fellow on my train who was sprawled out—he looked like he could mug someone really—sitting there with the shades on, the whole thing. And as I walked by him to go to the other side he rapped me on my leg and I said, Oh, come on, what's this going to be, trouble now? So I said, "What's happening, friend?"

He says, "I just want to thank you, man, for letting me feel like a human being."

And so I find that that's the reward.

CHAPTER 5

SIX INCHES FROM DEATH

> The hard part of this job, I'd say, is when you have
> to go down on the tracks. . . . Because when you
> go down there, your life's in your hands. You have
> to be very careful.
>
> *Jenny Mandelino*, Structure Maintainer[1]

Joe Caracciolo, a maintenance supervisor, once considered writing a book about his work on the tracks of the New York subway system. His proposed title: *Six Inches from Death*. "Because you're constantly about six inches away from the third rail. Every time you look up, the third rail is above you. You look to your side, the third rail is next to you."[2]

In addition to the 600 DC volts flowing through the third rail, there is the danger of moving trains. John Lorusso, a maintenance supervisor, remembers that the first time he was sent out on a track renewal job, "I was very scared. That first train looked like a huge, huge building coming at you."[3]

Harry Nugent, who had worked on track crews before he

became a conductor, concludes, "It was a great job, you know, if you love dirt, fear, and blood."[4]

More than anyone else in Transit, the men and women who work on the subway tracks enter into a perilous environment. Track workers use every sense to stay safe: they look for light from the train's headlight on the rails or the walls; they listen for the roar of the train; they feel the wind from an oncoming train against their skin. When they walk, they lift their feet to avoid tripping over tracks and ties. They are always alert for the third rail.

To stand on the track as a train goes by, with huge steel wheels that could easily crush you, is to feel like a dwarf. Underground, the passage of a train can make you fearful of a gruesome death in a dark, crowded place. On the elevated structures, if you look down at the tracks as the train goes by and see traffic buzzing beneath, you can feel vulnerable to being hit by a train, falling, and then being hit by a car.

Yet if the men and women who work on the tracks feel fear that they must learn to control, they also feel respect for the trains and the electricity that could claim their lives, camaraderie with their fellow work-crew members, and pride in doing a hard and dangerous job. Track workers, working in a system where past meets present, use tools as primitive as a sledgehammer and as sophisticated as a tamper, a huge computerized machine that fine-tunes the alignment of subway rails.

"You *respect* the third rail," says Richard Oakes, a deputy superintendent, "because if you don't respect it, you don't get a second chance."[5]

The need for caution is drilled into workers, much in the way that soldiers are trained to be alert in combat. As Paul Prinzivalli puts it,

> ‖‖‖ Sometimes you get so involved in your job . . . that you forget there's trains going around. And we are in a constant, hazardous territory. During a war . . . even the enemy gets tired and you have a little time where everybody takes their rest. But in a rapid railroad transit system, we have a rush hour that's rapid fire, and then

after the rush hour, we have what they call a "slower rapid fire," but still trains are running.[6] ⅢⅢ

General Superintendent Marty Kaiser reminds workers to be alert and listen for the warning sounds when they work on the track.

> ⅢⅢ You have to look, you have to listen, when you walk on the trackway, don't talk! The trains talk to you, you can hear the rails clicking, they talk to you, they tell you they're coming. You see that bright light now, you hear the noise—when you're out there you have to pay attention to what you're doing, and that's the most important thing.[7] ⅢⅢ

Yet even the sound of an oncoming train can be as much a hazard as a warning. As Harry Nugent explains,

> ⅢⅢ The worst accidents out there are stepping out of the path of one train into the path of another to avoid a train. . . . The sound of the train you see is masking the sound of the train you don't see. . . . So the thing on that job is you never take anything for granted. ⅢⅢ

Part of the solution is to develop a strong sense of teamwork, so that workers know where they are at all times and watch out for each other. "Actually," notes Richard Oakes, "after you've worked together with some people for a while, you know what the next move is without him even telling you." Earnis Briant, a superintendent of employees' facility rehabilitation, recalls the lessons a foreman teaches the first time a worker prepares to go out on the tracks.

> ⅢⅢ He will take you on the track and he will show you the hazards—the aprons, the switches—and he will tell you that this switch may be thrown from a distance, the guy that throws the switch doesn't know that you're there, so *you've* got to be careful about that. Because if you're walking and you're in the switch area and he throws the switch, it could catch your feet. And if your helper's with you, he's the only guy that can help you,

so you've got to be careful. . . . And that guy's got to watch *you*, and you likewise got to watch *him*.[8] ⅢⅢ

The relations between the members of a work crew, notes assistant general superintendent Eric Schmidt, acquire the characteristics of a family. "Each one had to be treated a little different. Some guys would complain about everything, other guys wouldn't complain about anything. They're all individuals. But you become like a family because if you don't work together, everybody works much harder."[9] Emilio Robertino believes that work crews have to work at getting along. "Remember, you work with people more than you're with your family. You're with the people you work with forty hours a week."[10]

In a situation where lives depend on teamwork, a lapse by one crew member can have dire consequences—as Joseph Fox learned working with Jack Fahr [a pseudonym].

ⅢⅢ We were in a gang situation, that is, four or five people working on a track. And when you do that you usually put out flags, flags being lights that indicate to the motorman that there is a group of people working on the track. And you have a flagman who is maybe 100, 200 feet in approach to where the actual work is taking place. And so we had Jack out there and he was supposed to flag for us.

And of course, I don't know what happened to Jack, but the next thing we looked up and about 100 feet in front of us was a train coming down. Four of us at the time just jumped out of the way of the train. And the train went by, and he was going at a fairly slow speed, but it was still very scary. And if I had caught Jack, he would not be alive today. I might be up doing time. He had taken an early lunch and never told us.

One of the things that usually takes place—it's probably done in a lot of situations—is that if you have a group of men and you have one guy that really doesn't fit in, you give him the most menial job. But in the case of a flagman, it's a menial job, it's a boring job, but it's an important job. So Jack always had problems

with the mechanics and the circuits. Jack was like an
outsider. We put him out with the flag. . . . It's an
important job, but it is more important to have skilled
people work together so that the job can be completed
properly. And unfortunately, Jack almost killed all of
us.[11] ▥

A stranger saved Paul Prinzivalli in the tunnels.

▥ I was walking along the track at Fourteenth Street
and Eighth Avenue on a special Superintendent inspec-
tion, and as I'm walking along, I got so preoccupied
[with] what I was writing down, that I forgot all about
trains. Really.

I'm starting to write, write, write, write, write; I had
my lamp under this arm and I had the clipboard, and
I'm looking at it and writing, writing—and all of a
sudden I hear a loud scream. I'll never forget that.
"Look out!" A frantic scream.

I looked up, and if you know the south end of
Fourteenth Street and Eighth Avenue, there's a sharp
high-speed curve there. When I looked up, the train
already was on the trailing end of the curve, just ap-
proaching the platform, and I was three-quarters in the
station, walking along the middle of the track, near the
third-rail side, when I heard that scream. I looked up
and I heard this loud SHHHHH!—that was the train
operator putting his train in emergency. I made one
leap, went over the third rail protection coverboard,
into that niche, and three cars went by me before the
train came to a final stop. In other words, he'd slowed
down but skidded. I couldn't talk—that was the biggest
shock I ever had—so then the train operator went from
car to car looking, finally he opened up the window,
and there I am in the niche and I looked up at him.
And he says, "Are you all right?"

Words couldn't come out of my mouth. I says,
"Yeah, I'm OK. Don't worry, I'm going to get to the
phone after you leave and I'll inform the Command

Center that it was my fault that you went into emergency. If there's any passenger injuries, I will assume
responsibility because I forgot you were coming."

He said, "Thank God." He felt relieved, and he took
his train out.

I'm getting my bearings now, and I'm resisting
walking on the track again. And I stood there a while,
to get my bearings. And I see this black man over there:
"Man," he says, "I never seen a man fly so fast," he says.
"I'm the one that yelled."

I said, "Oh, God bless you." I says, "Thank you very
much. You saved my life! I owe you and I'll always
remember that." Now, he could have minded his
business—I would have been a dead man today.

So from then on, I says, I can never discriminate
against the opposite race. Everyone is created equal.   ⁙

Danger teaches other lessons. A close call on the tracks made
Marty Kaiser more cautious.

⁙   I was working up in a Harlem River tube, that's up
on the Jerome Avenue line, and I was repairing pipes
down in a pit where all the water comes in that's
pumped out to the street. And I was down there and a
train was coming and they told me, "Just stay down
there," and they put the grates back on top of me and
they said, "As soon as the train passes we'll open it up."

And the pumps were not working because that's why
we were working down there. And I was down there,
and the train came over the top of me, and the water
started filling up, and the train stopped and got stuck
there, and I couldn't get out. And there was no way—I
couldn't lift up the grating because it's all electrical
above me, the car is above me. Maybe it wasn't as long
as it seemed, but to me it seemed forever.

And the water was building up and I had these high
boots on and the water came up above the top of the
boots and was going into my shoes. Now if this train
got stuck there, that would have been the end of me. I

would have drowned, number one. Number two, even
if I didn't drown and the water came up high enough
that it would have hit the contact rail, I would have
been electrocuted.

But anyhow, the train moved and they opened up
the grate and I got out. I would never do that again, I
would never expect anybody to do that again. . . . This
job is a very, very dangerous job. ⅢⅢ

The knowledge that transit workers acquire in the tunnels is
also put to use saving passengers. Paul Prinzivalli was doing
track maintenance north of Jay Street/Borough Hall when he
spotted some sailors walking down the track.

> ⅢⅢ They walked from High Street with their back to
> the train movement, and they were half drunk, walking
> along the middle of the track—it's a miracle—thank
> God we seen them, and thank God we removed them
> from the track in time: an A Train leaving High Street
> would have killed them. ⅢⅢ

Sometimes bad luck, inattention, or an accident strikes with
terrible consequences. Richie Triolo notes,

> ⅢⅢ A lot of people think that the danger in the tunnels
> is the third rail. That's the thing, "Oh, the third rail.
> The third rail."
>
> I know where the third rail is. So you just avoid it.
> But the thing that kills most transit workers, not all of
> them, is the trains. Because if you're working in the
> tunnels, if two trains are coming, you only hear one
> because one sound dominates another one. A friend of
> mine got killed down there. He came in third in Mr.
> America, a bodybuilder. One Monday, he goes down,
> the first tunnel he was in, boom, he got hit by a train.
> Twenty-five-year-old. Young guy. Nice guy. This was
> in '75. That was a whole tragedy. He was going to get
> married in six months. . . .
>
> A friend of mine just got killed; in fact, we started
> the same day together. We started April 1970. . . . He

got killed down Astor Place. Funny thing, he left the lighting department because he said, he can get off the tracks, because the tracks are dangerous. And he went to the telephone department. When crossing from one platform to the other one, him and his partner went across the tracks. . . . The train's coming around, they probably heard one train and they stepped out of the way of one train, they stepped onto the tracks of another train. Boom.

And I talked to him like a few days before because I hadn't seen him. . . . I said, "How you doing?"

He said, "I'm staying here four more years. I'll be fifty . . ." and boom. I'll never forget that.[12]   ‖‖‖

Marty Kaiser also lost a friend on the tracks, a man he talked into going to work in Transit. He worked in a track gang in Queens.

‖‖‖   And we still don't know what happened to him. The man lived right across the street from me. A train hit him. They think he dropped a pencil, bent down to pick it up, and he wasn't thinking what he was doing, and a train got him, killed him. I was to his wake. I still talk to his father and his mother and his sister. They don't blame me for it; it's just something that happened. But there's always danger here.   ‖‖‖

In the IRT, Paul Prinzivalli notes, workers had a habit of putting crosses on the tunnel wall to mark the spot where someone died. More reminders of deaths on the job circulated in the form of ghost stories, like the stories of a ghost at Grand Army Plaza in Brooklyn. "They'd say that you would hear him before a train comes," notes Prinzivalli. "The ghost will be walking along that track, because you'll hear click click click click. And after the train leaves you'll hear click click click. But this was magnetism from the train: the plates would get magnetized to the running rail as the train approached that area, and when he [the train] left the area, they would get demagnetized and drop down. So that was the ghost of Grand Army Plaza. There was no ghost."

Earnis Briant remembers a story that he learned on the A line in Manhattan near 145th Street.

> ‖‖‖‖ A guy came around back, and he says, "Look, there's something up there!"
>
> So we started looking, said, "What do you mean something's up there?"
>
> He said, "Look, look, something's dancing. You know a guy got killed around the curve that time."
>
> I says, "Aw, it's got to be something else. You can't see a thing like that." But the thing was waving like this. I got a little shaky—I didn't want to go.
>
> He said, "Come on, let's see what it is."
>
> So the closer we got to it, the more we knew what it was. It was smoke. There was a fire on the track, and the smoke was coming up and the smoke was just like this, and it looked like something strange. ‖‖‖‖

The ghosts that inhabit the tunnels of the subway are a fiction. But the homeless people who live there, despite the efforts of police and transit officials, are a real presence. Richie Triolo remembers walking through tunnels and seeing televisions, refrigerators, beds, and pictures on the walls set up by homeless people. Once he encountered a man cooking a chicken over a fire. Marty Kaiser recalls similar events.

> ‖‖‖‖ I was a plumbing foreman up in the Bronx at one time, and we were told about a smell coming out of a ventilator. We went there, we opened it up, and we went down in there and there was a man living there. In fact, he used to build a fire in the corner to do a little cooking, or to heat up whatever—and the smell was because the vent maybe was fifty feet long. He was using the furthest one as a bathroom. And the smell was starting to come up. To this day I don't know how he got the couch down in there, I still can't figure it out. . . .

But we broke up everything, we took it out, we threw disinfectant down in there, and there were cockroaches down in there and the water bugs and it was full of lice. We didn't leave him anything. We just cleaned it all out, we got a truck there, broke everything up, fumigated the place with bleach and ammonia to kill off the vermin, and we threw it on the truck and got rid of it all. I guess he never went back, I really don't know. |||||

Besides the "mole people" who live underground, animals also live in the tunnels. Lionel Bostick recalls dogs on the tracks.

||||| And it's an awful thing, because . . . I've seen a dog run for miles in front of a train, and he doesn't run that fast, so the train isn't going to run him over and the train just drags behind him. And I've seen one time they called up about two or three stations ahead, and they had people on the tracks trying to apprehend the dog, but nobody really wanted to get the dog because the dog is down there, you don't know if the dog is a mad dog or not. So they just tried to really shoo him out of the path of this train. So the dog goes and jumps over into the area of another train. And if he jumps over and a train is at full speed, he's in serious trouble. Not only will the train kill him, but if he tries to get out of the way and hits the third rail he's gone. There's many dead animals down there, mainly dogs.[13] |||||

Marty Kaiser recalls wild subway cats, particularly the ones he encountered working at the 239th Street garbage dumps. There, helpers carry the garbage out of the trains and put it into dump trucks that take it to landfill areas.

||||| And to keep the rats down, the Transit Authority used to pay so much money for cat food and ice to keep the cat food, but over the years I guess the money became less and the cats became more, and the cats would practically attack you for a frankfurter when you pulled it out of this hopper car. The little teeny kittens

were like wild things—you could never touch one, and if they were hungry and a hot dog came out of that hopper car and that thing saw it he'd hiss at you with his claws out and he'd bite you for that hot dog. ⅢⅢⅢ

CHAPTER 6

LAW AND ORDER

> You wouldn't live in a house next to a railroad
> track, understand? Here, you are doing one-third
> of your life every day in that type of noisy envi-
> ronment, which is what the subways are all about.
> Hot in the summer, cold in the winter. Everybody's
> problem that comes into the subway, you're going
> to meet.
>
> *Officer John Maye*[1]

I t is a strange and subterranean world: maddeningly crowded at one hour and eerily empty the next, its air heavy with steel dust ground from the wheels of subway trains. Beyond the platforms stretches a labyrinth of tunnels where a criminal can hide, all of them threaded by a third rail that can electrocute police officers and lawbreakers alike. For most people it is not a place to linger, but it is the accustomed workplace of the 2,775 officers of the New York Police Department Transit Bureau.

"I think it is one of the most stressful jobs in police work," says Officer Maye, who patrolled the transit system for thirteen years before becoming an employee relations officer.

||||| It's stressful because you are working in a climate where you have no relationship with really any of the passengers. We handle a transient population. They get on the train; they get annoyed if they don't get to their proper destination in a decent amount of time. You could be having a tussle with several culprits who are maybe assaulting somebody else or trying to rip somebody off and if the train came in, those passengers who are there will not assist you. They get on that train and get the hell out of there. Housing cops work with tenant organizations, store owners work with cops too. So here we have a transient population. . . . The relationship we have with the riding public depends upon the mood they're in when they get up in the morning. |||||

Lieutenant Squad Commander Carolyn Burke agrees.

||||| I think, in fact, the hardest police job in the state of New York is the transit police. Because at least 80 to 90 percent of the time, you're by yourself. Probably 60 percent of the time your radio works, and the other 40 percent it doesn't work because of the structure of the Transit Authority itself—in the subways, the steel and the cement blocks the messages. So you are by yourself when you are working in uniform, and I don't think any other police department does that as much as we do. And you're locked in, you're in a closed environment. So I think it is the most difficult job. I always say we're the Marines.[2] |||||

As Lieutenant Burke explains, subways traverse vast stretches of the city, from the safest neighborhoods to the most dangerous. Every time an officer gets off a train to chase a suspect, he or she is in a different community.

Moreover, Transit Bureau officers wrestle with the problems that police officers confront above ground, especially the boredom that can change in an instant to furious action. They may also complain, as do many police officers, that politicians have tied their hands. As Captain Richard Marks says,

⁞⁞⁞⁞ I don't perceive anybody as being a police officer anymore. I think we're all public relations consultants. Now they spit at cops, they throw things at cops, they abuse them, and very little happens to these people who do it. We have officers out there, and crimes are committed right while they're there. People commit crimes in front of me: I walk around in a captain's uniform, I'm talking about nonserious crimes, but still—people walk through a gate while I'm standing there in uniform.

I was standing at Berry Street a couple of months ago and an eighteen-year-old young lady—I was by myself, my driver was down the street—she came up with her girlfriends, smoking a cigarette, opened the gate, walked through, walked right past me. I said, "Excuse me, miss, where are you going?"

She said, "Up on the train."

I said, "The hell you are. Don't we pay our fare when we come down here?"

And she says, "Oh, oh, oh!" and she sauntered back out slowly, smoking.

I said, "Put that damn cigarette out!" and she put it behind her back and refused to put it out until I got sterner with her, and then she put it out and she bought a token and she went through. And when my driver came up, I told him to go up and bring her down and give her a summons for smoking and one for not paying her fare. An eighteen-year-old Italian girl, very nasty. And here I am standing, the only person besides her and a girlfriend, and a clerk in the booth, I'm the only person standing there, and I'm standing in a captain's uniform with my gun on and she walks right through the gate and right past me.

This would not have happened thirty years ago,

when I started. People in this city just don't give a
damn about anything. They'll park their cars in bus
stops, they'll park in No Standing zones, in front of fire
hydrants; the McDonald's at 161st Street, Yankee
Stadium, is a classic example: the people that I've had
tagged in that bus stop are just incredible: doctors,
judges—people in our city just don't care. . . . Total
lack of discipline. And our politicians allow this.[3] ⅢⅢ

Like all police officers, the officers who work in the Transit
Bureau must transfer their learning from the Police Academy
to the world of the subways. For Transit Bureau officers, that
includes special training on how to work on subway tracks,
how to shut off power, how to protect themselves against the
third rail, and how to work with the public. Lieutenant Burke
observes,

ⅢⅢ   They teach you basic things at school—how to
defend yourself—but when it comes down to being on
a platform with somebody, and you're putting them
under arrest and they start fighting, none of those things
work. Once you're confident with your basic stuff, in
what you have to know and what you have to do,
anything that comes along you can do, or make a
decision about, because it all has a foundation. ⅢⅢ

Part of the job is learning to handle the authority that comes
with a badge. Officer Floyd Holloway, a patrolman and later
first vice-president of the Police Benevolent Association, spent
his first two weeks in uniform alongside an older officer.

ⅢⅢ   Well, they taught me not to be thin-skinned.
Because being young, I was a lot more aggressive in
terms of dealing with so-called bad guys, and I guess
showing dominance. I had the mentality that, when I
was given a post, it was my post and there was no one
that was going to dominate that post other than myself.
And they taught me that you can't be thin-skinned, you
have to go with the flow, so to speak. Because you may
be right, but if your actions precipitate something

which is greater, you hold that responsibility too. So right doesn't necessarily make might.[4] ⁓

At the same time, observes Officer Maye, police have to learn to balance the demands of underground law enforcement.

⁓ It's the only job in the world where you can go to work in the morning, think you did a tremendous job, and be locked up that night for what you thought was a necessary police action. . . . Police work becomes like a doctor: if you're not up on, in tune with, the new procedures, you're gonna get in a hell of a lot of trouble—you're going to have all malpractice suits and things like that. Police officers have to constantly keep on top of what's taking place in the federal government, the state government, and the city government. A practice that he has been using for years and years might have been now found to be illegal or against the Constitution of the United States. If he's still using it because it was past practice for him, he winds up in a lot of trouble. ⁓

At the same time, officers must remain alert. Maye explains,

⁓ Your first arrest may be a minor arrest, and as you progress in taking necessary police actions, you get more and more used to it. In fact, sometimes you get so used to it, you become careless in apprehending people, and you allow them to get the drop on you rather than your taking command of a situation. ⁓

Out of such experiences emerge transit police officers' stories about close calls, painful accidents, and dangerous arrests. Maye recalls an incident when he worked alone in plainclothes trying to stop the after-school gang activities of students.

⁓ Gangs would meet on the subway systems, where one train would pick up a group of another school's kids as it's going over its route, so [you have] two different schools meeting and sometimes clashing. I one time had to lock up a whole car. An entire car of a

subway train. That was the Lexington Avenue Number
6 train, the Pelham Bay line running up towards
Pelham Bay. It was between 96th Street and 103rd
where the outbreak took place. And I locked up the
whole car. I convicted them.   ⁞⁞⁞⁞⁞

To the public, police work is defined by dramatic shoot-
outs. In fact, a typical Transit Bureau officer, like his or her
counterparts in other departments, rarely if ever fires a pistol.
Still, in the difficult moments of the job, an officer confronts
moral and ethical problems that would confound a philoso-
pher. Captain Marks says,

⁞⁞⁞⁞⁞   When I first came to this district in 1971, we were
having many, many booth robberies: we had the old
wooden booths in those days, with the incandescent
light bulbs outside and the grillwork in the front, and
we had booth robberies, oh, God, coming out of the
ears. . . .
   I think in the month of August of 1971, we had
something like nineteen booth robberies in one month.
Which was a phenomenal number, because when I first
came on in 1959, if we had sixty booth robberies a year,
that was a lot. . . . And I told my officers here, to try
and motivate them, I'll give a bottle of whiskey, your
choice, to anybody who makes a good booth robbery
arrest. And I did give out a number of bottles, because
they did start making some good arrests.
   And in October of 1971, I was told there was a guy
who had robbed a number of booths on the lower
White Plains line—and he was still down there, and I
went down there, and I had an officer meet me at
Prospect. The robber had left Prospect, went to Jackson. And we got on a train, went down to Jackson, we
got off the train right in front of the booth, and the
clerk in the booth pointed outside, and he says, "He's
still out there and he's got a gun."
   So I was in civilian clothes, and my officer was in
uniform, and I felt that as soon as the robber sees him,

he'll run. So I says, "No, no, I'll go out; you stay in here."

So I went out and I came up behind him, I grabbed him, and I was ready to do battle if he wanted to, I said, "Don't make a move or I'll shoot you." And he turned and he started to run down the stairs, and I couldn't see his hands. So I shot him, and it killed him, a sixteen-year-old booth robber.

So, that's a war story. And that's the only time I ever fired a shot down here in anger, and it cost a young life. He lingered for six days in the hospital, finally died, and for eleven days he was unidentified. . . . Nobody even missed him; nobody was even looking for him. And then finally he was identified, and then they had a Grand Jury investigation, naturally—whenever a life is taken in New York City, you have a Grand Jury investigation—and they had invited the father of the youth to come to the Grand Jury, and he didn't even come. ⅢⅢ

Lieutenant Burke faced the usual challenges of policing as well as the challenge of being a woman on a mostly male force. She grew up in a family of police officers, took the police test in 1964 at the age of nineteen, and was hired two years later. At the beginning of her career, women officers were used only for special details, such as interviewing female victims of robberies or sex crimes and working as a decoy. She also worked with juveniles and female prisoners. For twelve years on and off, she had one male officer for a partner.

ⅢⅢ I guess in the beginning you're just afraid. You have all this authority, you've never had it before—it's a little strange. You can lock people up, take their freedom away from them.

I was twenty-one years old at a time when women weren't really into any of that type of stuff. From what I see of the young girls coming on now, they've been raised differently than I was, so . . . there's no problem with it. I think they have a problem relating to working with men. Some overreact and want to become mannish and tough, and you really don't have to be. You be yourself. ||||||

Lieutenant Burke learned that the ability to laugh was an important asset.

|||||| Luckily, my partner had a good sense of humor, so we always laughed. I guess it's gallows humor. One day when I was coming into work, I locked up a fourteen-year-old boy for exposing himself to me. He did it, I locked him up, and ten years later I was investigating a rape case—there was a series of them in the subway in Port Authority, which is at Forty-second Street. We came up with a suspect, and I looked at the picture, and I said, "Gee, this man looks very familiar to me." It was the same fourteen-year-old kid. He was twenty-four, but he had progressed into beating women and raping them. . . . In fact, he recognized me before I recognized him. ||||||

Lieutenant Burke and her partner developed a code system for use on subway platforms.

|||||| If I started whistling, he knew I had somebody I was watching. I always whistled "Winchester Cathedral" when there was somebody around that looked like they might do something. The prearranged signal was that I would pull on my collar, which was "we had a collar"—arrest somebody. He knew from where I was in the station and who I was watching. He could tell sometimes beforehand what was happening, just on the expression on my face. He might not even have been able to see the person I was watching. ||||||

As a woman, Lieutenant Burke faced unique challenges. Her regulation skirt was less than perfect for chases through backyards in Jamaica, Queens. And on cold days her exposed knees went blue from the cold.

There were so few female officers at the time that "when

you showed somebody your shield, either they were flabbergasted or they decided they were going to run away." Lieutenant Burke believes that she was probably challenged more often than a male officer. "If you backed down, of course, you lost. So you could never back down." More than once, she wrestled a suspect into submission on a subway platform.

For both men and women on the force, the hardships of underground police work did not always win them acclaim or recognition. The New York Police Department Transit Bureau evolved out of a force that first patrolled the city-owned IND line and was later expanded to patrol the IRT and BMT when they were taken over by the city in 1940. The original force had powers of arrest only on the IND line, which made them appear to be less-than-complete police officers. Not until 1947 did the subway police officers have legal status equal to that of the New York City Police Department, and even when they won it they still worked under the Police Department's supervision. The Transit Police Department became an independent entity in 1955, however, and grew in numbers until the mid-seventies, when the city's fiscal crisis led to layoffs, reductions by attrition, and a hiring freeze. Recurring proposals to merge the Transit Police Department and the New York City Police Department clouded the future of the Transit Police and hurt officers' morale.

Officer Holloway recalls a phrase that angered officers in the middle of the 1960s.

‖‖‖ There was a saying, "In the back, Transit." They felt as though whenever they went into a precinct, or whenever they had a condition, they were always last. They were considered stepchildren of the Authority. They got the leftovers. ‖‖‖

Among transit police officers, one response was to draw a sharp distinction—in their own minds—between themselves and the rest of the transit force. Captain Marks recalls,

‖‖‖ I was a transit worker and I've been a transit police officer. But I think it's the ultimate insult to tell the

average transit police officer that his fellow employee is
a train operator or a railroad clerk. For whatever strange
reason, and I really don't understand it, that seems to be
an insult to them. And I don't think it is, and it
shouldn't be. Because we're all here to work to-
gether. ||||||

The morale and performance of the Transit Police Department improved dramatically when Chief William Bratton led
the department from 1990 to 1992. Under his leadership, the
force adopted a highly active style of policing. Instead of waiting for calls for assistance before taking action against crime,
the Transit Police set out to prevent crime by attacking robbery, fare-beating, and general disorder. The department expanded patrols, decentralized decision making, improved radio
communications, and armed its officers with 9-mm semiauto-
matic pistols.

These tactics gave transit officers a solid record reducing crime
in the subways. Between 1990 and 1994 subway homicides went
down 70 percent, rapes 42 percent, and robberies 42 percent.
Officers who remember the gloomy days of the late seventies
came to serve on a force distinguished by spirit and a solid track
record; under the prodding of Mayor Rudolph W. Giuliani,
and despite complaints from some transit officers, the Transit
Police Department was merged with the New York City Police Department, becoming the Transit Bureau in 1995.[5]

The officers who police the buses and subways know they
have a difficult job. They also know how to find pride in their
work, as Officer Maye relates.

|||||| I don't think it's the fact that you can lock people
up that makes you any way powerful; it's the fact that
you are able to spot things that the average person
couldn't spot: the pickpocket, after a while. In the
school conditions, although we watched for rowdyism
and discons [disorderly conduct offenses] and assaults . . .
you also watched for the pervert who tries to take
advantage of children on the train, things like that.
Their motions, their actions, the look in their eyes, and

the child they are bothering with, the look on her face, you know, tells you that something is going on. Now you maneuver yourself in a position to see what's happening and take care of that situation. All of this . . . is the thrill of knowing that they are doing something wrong, and that you are removing them for some small period of time. ⅢⅢ

CHAPTER 7

DRIVING BUSES

You get on your bus in the morning with your personality but the first person you pick up has an entirely different personality. So if you don't want to cross swords with this person you have to adjust your personality to meet that person's personality. So if you carry a thousand people a day, you're adjusting your personality a thousand different times.

Fred McFarland, Bus Driver[1]

As he approached retirement, bus driver Scotty McShane recalled the advice of one of his first transit instructors, an old Irishman who said that a bus driver should always "get the people that you're going to be carrying to like you and to feel that they want to help you."

⁞⁞⁞⁞⁞ And it stuck in my mind. So that's the way I work. I greet all my passengers. A lot of guys they laugh at me but, hey, I greet all my passengers. I don't care who they are. School kids, whatever. I say, "Good

morning," "good afternoon," whatever. I wish them a
good day when they get off. ⦚

McShane's rule is founded on a basic fact of his job: driving
a bus is hard work; it is even harder if the people you carry are
hostile to you and unwilling to stand by you in troubles rang-
ing from an accident to an unruly passenger to a breakdown.
The pressure is relentless. Unlike other jobs, McShane explains,
a bus driver cannot get up and take a break when the tension
and work build up.

> ⦚ What people don't realize is that when you're
> behind that wheel your mind and your eyes . . . are
> constantly going because you got to watch anything
> that's in front of you, anything that's parked, anything
> behind you, the people, you have to watch the people,
> you don't know where they're going to come from, out
> in between trucks, between cars. Your mind and your
> eyes are constantly alert. And that's tiring, believe me.
> . . . It's an exhausting, mental, exhausting job. ⦚

The difficulty of coping with traffic is not readily apparent
to passengers, McShane says.

> ⦚ I had a woman sit next to me and I cut a cab off at
> the bus stop, which is what we're told to do; if it's at a
> bus stop you got to get in front of him to cut him off,
> and this woman says to me, "You know, they have to
> make a living too."
>
> And I says, "Yes, ma'am, but that's a bus stop. If
> people want to get off and on, he's keeping me from
> getting to the sidewalk. What if I went behind him and
> he took off? Now there's room, somebody else can
> come between me and the curb."
>
> She says, "I think you're still too hard on these poor
> drivers. They have to make a living too."
>
> So I says to her nicely, "Sit right where you're
> sitting, look through that windshield until you get off
> and put yourself behind the wheel. Think as a driver."

She got off the bus, she says, "I wouldn't take this job for a million dollars." ⫿⫿⫿

In addition to the traffic, drivers also know that they—for better or for worse—are the Transit Authority's most visible ambassadors. "You have to take a lot of abuse," says McShane. "If the company makes a mistake the people don't go to the source of the mistake; they come to the operator because he's a representative of the company."

The solution, in addition to driving well, is to get the passengers on the driver's side. "Every day is precious," says McShane. "And if I'm going to have to be behind the wheel I might as well make it enjoyable." Once, at Christmas time, he drove his bus in a Santa Claus suit. People waved, children posed for pictures in his lap, and a television station interviewed him.

More typically, during a snowstorm, for example, McShane will joke with his passengers.

⫿⫿⫿ The people will be down, bad day, I say, "Attention folks, announcement from the MTA. Right away, Announcement from the MTA. If we hit an iceberg and the bus starts to sink the life preservers are under your seats. But I don't go down with the bus. I'll be the first one out." And they bust out laughing. It makes the day a little easier. Things like that. You have to. If you don't, you're crazy. ⫿⫿⫿

In a city famed for its anonymity, drivers and passengers can actually become fixtures in each other's lives. McShane drove on Twenty-third Street for thirteen or fourteen of his twenty years as a bus driver. He got to know his passengers, including a Jewish family, and watched their children grow up. "When they came back from Israel for a visit, they bought me back a tee shirt and it had on it 'State of Israel' and on the back it had 'Scotty McShane.'"

Fred McFarland befriended passengers on a late-night bus run.

⫿⫿⫿ I used to come up to Thirty-fourth Street and

Sixth Avenue. One night I came up, it was like 2:30 in
the morning and I see a bunch of people running down
Thirty-fourth Street. So I say, should I take off or
should I wait? Maybe somebody needs some help, you
know. What it was was a bunch of elderly women.
Now they get on the bus and they say, "Oh, you're so
sweet, you waited."

They were the cleaning women. They used to call
them "the scrubbies." They were the cleaning women
in the Empire State Building. So we got to know each
other. There was like eight or nine of them. This is
going back twenty-six years ago.

My trip there was my last trip. I wasn't going anyplace at three in the morning but home and going to
bed. . . . I knew they were coming down the block at a
certain time and if they missed my bus they had like an
hour wait for the next bus. So, I waited for them. I
mean, I still got a ton of time because there's no traffic.

These women got to be like mothers to me, all black
women, right, but they got to be like a mother to me. I
mean they knew my name, they knew my children,
they knew this, they knew that.

When I got a little more seniority I was able to
change runs. Now I could pick something finishing
three hours earlier. Boy, I was big time now. I told the
girls, I says, "Next Friday is my last Friday here. . . ."

"Oh, you can't do this. We're going to write letters.
We got to keep you with us."

I said, "No, you can't do that." I says, "I want to go
home and see my kids a little bit, right?"

"Oh, you can't leave us."

Well, as it was, that Friday night they got on the bus,
very, very quiet, very, very solemn, you know. I said,
"Come on girls, let's start singing something. I'm not
dying, I'm just leaving. But I'll still be uptown. I'll see
you."

So, we proceeded uptown and one of them, I'll

never forget her, Mary her name was, she was about four foot nothing, and she come up and she had a card and she says, "Here, Freddy, this is from the girls." So, I says, "Oh, thank you."

I figured it was a thank you card and I never opened it until I started home. In the thing was all their signatures, a "thank you very much," and a fifty-dollar bill. Twenty-six years later I have this card and the same fifty-dollar bill.   ⁙

Other passengers are memorable because they create problems that drivers have to solve. McFarland recalls one such incident.

⁙   It was extremely cold, it was during the winter, I was driving one of our older-type buses because we didn't have these newer buses, but the heat was very good. . . . I was making my first trip down, I was working the Number 7 line, Fourteenth Street and Union Square. It was a Friday about 4:30 in the afternoon, very, very cold so I had the heat blasting.

So a girl gets on the bus. She's carrying a big box that says, "Schweppes," so I figured well, this girl's going to have a real great time for the weekend, she's got a whole case of Schweppes. . . . I pick up a few other people and we start to go across Fourteenth Street and turn up Sixth Avenue and I got about three blocks up Sixth Avenue and all of a sudden I hear, "Oh my God."

So instantly I brought the bus to a stop and I turned around and in this box she had a big cat. I didn't know there was a cat. Otherwise she wouldn't have been able to get on the bus. The cat evidently hadn't gone to the bathroom in six weeks. This cat went to the bathroom and it splashed on her coat and on two seats.

Needless to say, with the heat and cat urine does stink pretty bad. Our radios were working at that time, I called control; control says, "Where's your next dispatcher?"

I says, "Thirty-fourth Street."

He says, "Well, bring the bus to Thirty-fourth Street and see what he wants to do."

Now, meanwhile . . . I'm still in service, he's not telling me to go out of service. I had an elderly Jewish woman sitting directly across. She was the comedian of the whole scene. Everybody that got on the bus she would say, "Bubbi, don't sit there. A cat made a peepee." And this is what the woman kept saying over and over.

Now, I got to Thirty-fourth, no dispatcher. Dispatcher says to me on the radio, he says, "Where's your next dispatcher?"

"Sixty-seventh and Broadway." Meanwhile, I had just finished lunch. With the heat and the cat urine, the lunch started to rise. Now I'm opening windows.

We get up to Sixty-seventh, I got three people, the elderly Jewish woman is still with me, and she's telling everybody, "Don't sit there, the cat made a peepee." Meanwhile no foot dispatcher. He was either on break, or a meal or wherever he was, right?

I call control again, "Take it to 106th Street."

I says, "Whoa, pal, I can't go any further because I'm pretty sick now. I'm nauseous from the urine and stuff."

He says, "Okay, leave it there."

Now, you think that I had just robbed Fort Knox because within about five minutes five radio cars were on top of me. "What happened? What happened?" And I told them a woman had a cat, you know, in a box and there's two big puddles of urine in the seats.

Well, the dispatcher says, "How bad could it be?" Now meanwhile I had gotten out of the bus, put my jacket on, kept the doors closed.

He opened the door. The man actually fainted from the smell that hit him in the face. He fainted dead away. Two guys had to pick him up.

They revived him and he says, "What died in your

bus?" "Look," he says, "open all the windows. I'll have a radio car follow you." He says, "Take it up to the garage."

I says, "Okay." Now I get up to 106th Street and there's two other bosses sitting on the corner.

"What happened, Freddy?" I told him. One guy gets on the bus. Now, with all the windows open he gets on the bus and he says, "I don't believe it," he says, "I never smelled anything so bad in my life." He goes in a bodega and he comes out with six cans of air freshener and he says, "As you drive just spray it over your shoulder, Fred."

So that's how we got the bus back to the garage, by spraying air freshener because this cat urinated in the bus. ▥

Another passenger involved McFarland in an episode that established the value of honesty and the kindness of strangers in New York City. McFarland recalls finding the wallet of a doctor from the Hospital for Joint Diseases. He called the doctor to tell him.

▥ This man did everything but kiss my ring. He says, "Give me your name, I'll send your kids gifts." . . . He wanted to give me anything. The main reason was there was a narcotics card in his wallet and if anyone ever found the wallet they could have forged his signature and got all the narcotics they wanted. P.S., he gave me his business card and he says to me, "If you need any medical attention whatsoever," he says, "don't hesitate to call me." He says, "If I can't get it done," he says, "I'll get somebody to do it for you."

To make a long story short, about four years after that my mother took a stroke. Now, we knew she was going to die, basically, it was a very bad blood clot in the brain. The family was at Jamaica Hospital, we were all pretty upset.

And then I said to myself, "Gee," I says, "I got a

doctor's card that I found his wallet four years ago. It doesn't hurt to give him a call." I called this doctor up, he remembered me right away.

"You are the bus driver that found my wallet," he says. "What's your problem?" So I told him. He says, "All right, tomorrow morning at Jamaica Hospital there will be Doctor so and so. . . . He's the top neurosurgeon in the country." He says, "He will come and check your mother out from stem to stem. And if he can't save her life he will tell you."

I says, "What's this going to cost?"

He says, "No charge. This one's on me. . . ."

I was sitting in Jamaica Hospital with my family around the clock, because my mother was pretty bad. At 9:30 in the morning over the PA system, "Mr. McFarland please come to the Administration Office." The doctor that he had sent was in the Administration Office. And he introduced himself and he said, "I will go upstairs and I'll check your mother out."

He came downstairs about four hours later and he says, "Look, only God can save your mother. The blood clot is in such a position that if I operate it will move and it will kill her faster." He says, "Let her stay in God's hands. If you want me to go in, I'll go in. But I'll give you no guarantee at all."

I said, "No, thank you very much."

And he says, "By the way, our mutual friend says, 'Anytime you need us again just call.'"

And that's only because I found a man's wallet. And, I tell you, I felt fantastic about this. I mean, I had a man that was a top neurosurgeon look at my mother, which I could have never afforded anyway, all because of driving a bus and making a friend. That's why memories that I have, they can give me a million dollars and they can't give me better memories than I have.　〰〰

Of course, not all passengers provide drivers with such pleasant memories. Sometimes, the unpleasant incidents have a racial dimension. Dick Hinton, an African American, once challenged a woman because she got on the bus with four children and put in twenty cents—even though they were old enough to pay.

   ⅠⅠⅠⅠⅠ I asked her if the children were with her—she would have to pay for them—and she cursed me out. I was brand-new on the job and I only thought I was doing the right thing and I took a lot of abuse. She called me out a lot of names, she called me a lot of nasty names, asked me what happened to the Irish drivers and the Italian drivers, they never made her pay for her kids. Now you black so-and-so's come on the job and you think you own the company and blah, blah, blah.

   I kind of took low to it because I wasn't used to it, you know. Before that I drove an ambulance and I didn't have them problems. So I swallowed it and I got through with it. Of course, my mother helped me there. She told me before I got the job, "When you're dealing with people you have to learn to see and don't see." And that stayed in the back of my mind for years driving. Because people are people.[2] ⅠⅠⅠⅠⅠ

Hinton recalls,

   ⅠⅠⅠⅠⅠ I had two instances where I was called "nigger" on the bus behind the wheel and it didn't rest easy with me. I was very upset. I think I was more upset because I couldn't get him. . . . Punch him in the eye or something like that. You know you can't do it. You got to sit there and take that crap. In my twenty-two years one time I was spit upon. ⅠⅠⅠⅠⅠ

Yet for all the problems that passengers cause for drivers, they also provide indispensable help in difficult situations. McFarland recalls,

   ⅠⅠⅠⅠⅠ I was at the Port Authority and I had my regular passengers getting on. . . . I had this one guy get on and say, "I'm a veteran, I don't have to pay."

   I said, "I'm sorry, sir, you have to pay," which is

what the company says—you have to acknowledge it.
. . . The guy started to give me a hard time. He started
to give me a lot of lip. He's going to do this, he's going
to do that.

Three passengers got up and threw him off the bus. I
didn't have to touch him. Three passengers that ride my
bus regularly, and these were big guys, they worked for
Con Edison, they got up, first they asked him, "Would
you please get off the bus?"

He said, "I ain't getting off the bus, nobody's going
to make me get off the bus."

They grabbed him and literally threw him off the
bus, I mean threw him. He didn't hit one of those three
steps. This is what passengers can do to back you up.
You get in a problem, they can back you up. |||||

McShane also once relied on a passenger to defuse an
incident.

||||| I picked up these school kids and this girl came on,
she had a radio and it was blasting and I said—I didn't
ask her to turn it off, I remember this very distinctly—I
said, "Miss, would you please turn it down low." And
she reached over and she turned it off.

Well, her macho boyfriend, he reached over and he
says, "Nobody tells us what we can do." He turned it
on blasting. . . . And he looked at me and I was looking
at him and I pulled up, I wasn't going to move.

I pulled up the hand brake and I said, "Sir, I asked
the young lady, would she turn it down and she turned
it off. Why do you have to turn it up? You know it's
illegal to play the radio on the bus."

And the guy says, "None of your business." And he
called me a few names.

So I said, "Well, I'll tell you. I'm not moving the bus
until the radio is turned off. You're not keeping me
here. I'm getting paid. You're keeping all the rest of
these people here."

He says, "I don't care."

With that, this guy, black guy, got up out of the seat
and, I'm telling the truth, when he turned around and
faced that kid I couldn't see the kid and I couldn't see
his girlfriend, that's how big this guy was. And all he
said was, "Turn off that mother f–ing radio or I'm
going to shove it up your ass."

And I heard, "click," and I said, "Thank you, sir,"
put the bus back in gear, put down the hand brake, and
continued. If you get the passengers on your side there
is so much trouble that you can avoid. ⦚

Passengers, McShane explains, can also be helpful witnesses
when an accident happens.

⦚ I was crossing Twenty-third Street, it was about
seven o'clock. It was raining like crazy and Twenty-
third Street at that time was cobblestones. I had the
green light, I'm behind a cab, we're going across,
somebody whistled, the cab stopped dead, smack dead
in the middle of Twenty-third Street. No way I could
stop and not hit him. So I hit him. Goes through a
slick. He slid across Twenty-third into the bus stop on
the other side.

So . . . I turned around, I said, "Look, I don't know
if any of you saw the accident. If any of you did I
would appreciate some names and telephone numbers
so that I could have witnesses that the guy stopped dead
in the middle of Twenty-third Street." I had seventeen
signatures, seventeen telephone numbers. And knowing
my passengers, I knew a few of them were in the back
of the bus. They couldn't even see the accident if their
life depended on it. But they were willing to go and say
they saw the accident and it was the cab's fault.

When I came for the hearing the guy says, "You hit
the front of the bus." In this system you're wrong if you
hit anything with the front of the bus, you're wrong. So
I went in there and the guy says, "Hey, we're going to
have to find you at fault. You hit the cab with the front
of your bus." Even though I explained the situation.

The guy says, "You still hit him. You should have been able to have control and been able to stop."

I says, "Well, I'll tell you what . . . I have my seventeen witnesses—"

He says, "You have seventeen witnesses?"

I says, "Yes."

"Oh," he says, "they're willing to say that it was the cab's fault."

I says, "Yeah."

He says, "Okay, dismissed. Not at fault." ⅢⅢ

The biggest problem for the driver, according to McFarland, is management. McFarland, a veteran driver, believes that many recent managerial developments in the Transit Authority are moving the system away from the flexibility of past years, when drivers enjoyed more autonomy and freedom of action on the road.

ⅢⅢ   I hope and pray that this system doesn't deteriorate to zero. But the way it's headed in my personal feelings is they're going to hurt this system very bad. Because they won't turn it back to the man who knows what he's doing, which is the guy on the street. Which is your operator. He's your best source of information. He's your best source of knowing what's going on.

When drivers and dispatchers work together in a flexible setting, they can alter service on their own to compensate for fires or other unexpected delays. This new management won't let you do that. Everything is by the book. And you can't run a road by the book. ⅢⅢ

Nevertheless, McFarland believes that management does some things right, such as giving out driving awards, which boost morale and give drivers something to work for.

ⅢⅢ   You got guys that are striving out there not to have an accident so they get a ring or they get a watch or they get a pin. And if you walk around the swing room you'll see guys walking around with these things all around their lapel because it says 21, 22, 23, 24 Years No Accidents. It's a service award. It's a good feeling. And that's what this management has capitalized on, and I hope they keep capitalizing on it. ⫼

McFarland also values the compliments and thanks that come from passengers, whose lives randomly intersect with his own while he is driving his bus.

⫼ I had an incident where I got a commendation letter, going back about five years ago. I was sitting at Thirty-fourth Street and Lexington Avenue going westbound. A heavy-set black woman was crossing the street. She had just gotten off a Thirty-fourth Street cross-town going the opposite way. She had a baby in her arm and another one she was walking with. She had a transfer in her hand. She was going to get the Lexington Avenue bus going downtown. As she proceeded across in front of my bus the transfer blew out of her hand so I beeped my horn to point that she dropped the transfer because she didn't realize it.

She stopped on the other side of the street and she proceeded to go and get her transfer. The light changed. The little boy started crying, "Mommy, Mommy, please don't go. The bus is going to run you over and kill you and I'll have no Mommy." Now, I wasn't going anyplace.

But I open my door in the middle of the street which I'm not supposed to do, and I ripped off a transfer and I handed it to the lady. I says, "Here, ma'am."

"You're a God," she says.

I said, "No I'm not. I'm just a human being."

She wrote a letter in, a four-page letter. She didn't know my name. She didn't even know my badge number because she wasn't on my bus. She just remembered my bus number. . . . She put in the letter I had made her day. ⫼

Twenty-third Street cross-town buses.

CHAPTER 8

SHOPS AND YARDS

What we do is anything that is necessary for
repair, overhaul, and cleaning the subway car.
Mike Lombardi, Chief of Service Delivery[1]

There was a large element of irony in Mike Lombardi's
old job as assistant chief mechanical officer of the "B"
subdivision in the New York Transit Authority: when
he did it well, it was invisible. The trains looked clean and ran
on time and people took them for granted. When they broke
down, people noticed.

Lombardi, who worked at the 207th Street Maintenance
Shop, was part of a vast network of skilled transit workers. They
are mechanics and electricians who repair subway cars; iron
workers who maintain the structures for the els; sheet-metal
workers and blacksmiths who make ventilation ducts and repair tools; carpenters who build frames for pouring concrete;
car painters; graphic artists and printers who create signs. They
labor in an archipelago scattered across the face of the city,
from the 240th Street Maintenance Shop in the Bronx to the

Car Equipment Coney Island Maintenance Shop in Brooklyn.
The repair work that keeps trains running unavoidably puts transit workers at risk of injury. In the repair yards, they labor in a dangerous setting. With all their heavy machinery and electrical lines repair shops are covered with warnings: "Danger Hard Hat Area," "Safety Glasses Must Be Worn at All Times," and "Danger High Voltage." The warning against high voltage is to protect workers against a problem they commonly discuss: "getting zapped," or being shocked with the 600 DC volts used to power the subway. George Havriliak recalls,

> ⁞⁞⁞⁞   A lot of times I got hit with the 600 volts. I got zapped. And I'll never forget the first time I got hit was when I was new in the game, and I was setting up for a test demonstration. Doug Tilton told me, "Go out and set up the cars," he gave me a schematic. And I didn't realize that something was a 600-volt potential. I got hit with it. I jumped out of that cab and I never said the "Our Father" so much or so fast in my life.[2]   ⁞⁞⁞⁞

Lombardi recalls his early days as an electrician, crawling under subway cars to connect and disconnect cables. He jokes, but the shock of 600 DC volts frightened him.

> ⁞⁞⁞⁞   I got hit by 600 volts a couple of times. . . . It gives you a burst of energy for the next ten weeks. You get a charge out of it, so to speak.
>
> I was working on a car the first time I got hit. I had everything disconnected, all the electrical connectors that go into the car. I had a little sign up that said, "Do not bug this car." Bug means putting 600 volts on this car. I took out the fuses up in the panel, in the cab, just in case some moron came by and stuck this bug on the car, put the 600 on. I opened up a big knife switch, I took these fuses and stuck them in my pocket so I was safe. Because someone would have to go to great lengths to try to get this car energized.
>
> So I'm working on this car, and I needed a tool. It

was a 7/16 wrench. And I get out of this pit underneath this car, and I go fifteen minutes away to get this tool and come back. I only had another hour to finish this job before it's quitting time, and I had about two hours of work ahead of me, and I only had an hour to go. So I dug right back into it, not realizing that while I was away, somebody put the bug on, put the knife switch in, and replaced all the fuses up in the cab. Here I'm under there and all of a sudden, I get knocked up. My wrench disintegrated. I'm in the other end of the pit. I say, "How did I get here?" |||||

Lombardi has his own explanation for why he survived.

||||| I'm Italian. I think that's the reason. It's *pasta asciut'*. You eat a lot of *pasta asciut'*. No, I don't know why. Because I'm young and healthy, and I wasn't standing in water, and I had decent shoes on. I wasn't totally grounded. If I was leaning up against the subway car and working on it, it probably would have gone through my heart and killed me. It didn't grab a hold of me and keep me. It just knocked me down. It was a very frightening experience, but then, it's like getting off a roller coaster ride. It's like exhilarating after the adrenaline's going. It was like—great being alive. |||||

In conversations, senior transit workers say that safety procedures to prevent such accidents are much more strict today than in the past. Safe work habits have to be learned; when they are not learned, workers sometimes cover for each other with ironic results. As Vincent Ricciardelli, a superintendent, notes,

||||| So one of the items that a lot of people had a hard time with was helmets. And unless the front office—the big brass—enforced it, very rarely did anybody wear a helmet. But if somebody fell in the pit everybody would say, "In the pit!" And if the fall in the pit didn't kill him, the sixty-five helmets would, because if the

guy fell in the pit without wearing his helmet he would get written up for not wearing his helmet. So just to make sure that the guy didn't get written up everybody would just instinctively throw a helmet in the pit. So the guy would be laying in the pit with a broken arm and covering his head so that he wouldn't get hit with a helmet.[3] ⫶⫶⫶

Out of such shared dangers and work routines emerges a sense of camaraderie among repair shop workers. Sometimes it is expressed in jokes and initiation pranks used to mark newcomers' passage into the ranks of the regulars in the shop. Leonard Offner, train service supervisor, recalls that some people would tell new workers to look for Track Y35.

⫶⫶⫶ You didn't know what the guy was talking about. You'd be all over the place looking and then you'd come back and tell him you can't find it and the yard master would be cracking up. Because there's no such track.[4] ⫶⫶⫶

James Davitt, a superintendent, recalls that newcomers had to accept pranks gracefully. Eddie Pazoga, he remembers, was a major prankster.

⫶⫶⫶ He would tell the new guy, "You got to go up to Mr. Dorst's office to be demagnetized." One by one they filed in there. And you knew exactly what had happened because Jeanette would get on the loud-speaker and say, "Eddie Pazoga, report to Mike Dorst's office." And there would be some poor pigeon standing there and then he would walk in and deny everything of course. Now you had to find out if the guy would rat out Eddie for saying he sent him to Mike Dorst's office. So if the guy didn't rat him out he was OK. ⫶⫶⫶

At other times, the sense of camaraderie between repair shop workers is expressed in simple recognition of a job well done. For Joseph Allotta, such thanks makes his job worthwhile.

⫶⫶⫶ I like best what I am doing right now. I'm working

in this Coney Island Yard, Tower B, they call it. And I love it. You know why? When I do something, it shows. After I wash that floor, it looks so nice and clean, even if sometimes two hours later it will get dirty. But for that two hours, the place looks very nice. . . . What I like the best of the whole thing is that people that I work with come over to me and always say how nice a job you're doing. And that means more to me—I know it's going to sound stupid or crazy—than if they put five dollars a week more in my envelope, because that makes me feel good that I'm doing my job. And that's it.⁵ ▥

Transit workers who took part in the fight against graffiti, which appeared in the subways in the early 1970s and soon became a metaphor for anarchy in the city and its transit system, take pride in their contributions. Although the scratches in subway windows are a reminder that their job is not over, transit workers see the battle against graffiti as a success story. Chief Mechanical Officer A. R. Goodlatte recalls the struggle.

▥ We attacked the graffiti problem first because it was obviously the easiest thing to attack. We had six thousand broken-down cars covered with graffiti. We knew darn well we couldn't fix those six thousand cars as fast as we could clean up the graffiti. Because to fix them was a major proposition. To clean up the graffiti was more a logistics and strategy-type process where you said, "All right, let's take it a bit at a time, bite off a chunk, get it under control, go onto the next chunk." . . . We wanted to establish a foothold. We wanted to say to the public and the politicians that we can do something.

We took on the graffiti and we set a goal the first year and we made it. And then the second year we had a big ceremony where we hit three thousand cars. That was a key turning point because it happened just before the state legislature was getting ready to vote on our second capital program and I think at that time people were starting to say (like the mayor, the governor, and many people) that these guys have half the fleet cleaned up. They set the goal, they achieved the goal, and they're now halfway there. Let's give them a chance to finish this job with the second five-year capital program. I really believe that was a very important part of us establishing credibility.[6] ||||||

Despite some initial mistakes, the day-to-day tactics of the fight emerged. Richard Buffington, a superintendent for car repair, recalls the campaign.

|||||| We were painting the cars white. Whoever the hell came up with that color, that was just . . . inviting somebody: that is a blackboard for somebody. And you can see the kids up on the hill, right, waiting for us to leave because they had the spray cans and it was "the trail." We used to call it "the Ho Chi Minh trail." They used to come right down to Broadway Yard, just climb a little fence, all right, come down, and then climb up the structure and they were in the yard.[7] ||||||

Over time, as Buffington recalls, successful strategies emerged. In part, that meant spending enough money to do the job.

|||||| First of all, they hired more people to take care of the graffiti. I don't know how many millions they spent in barbed wire and razor wire to keep kids out of the yards, all right. So, we were lacking security; with the money they built security. We were lacking personnel to clean; with the money we hired more people to clean, all right. We put supervision with them, made sure they were productive. And each train that went to the station terminals, it would get swept, mopped if it need be. If somebody threw up or spilled something it would be mopped up, otherwise just swept. Graffiti had to be off the car in forty-eight hours. The car was taken out of service if [the graffiti] couldn't be taken off. And that was it. And it is still working. ||||||

The vast scale of transit repair yards and the operations conducted there can obscure the human factors of the workplace. For Mike Lombardi, a visit from then-MTA Chairman Robert R. Kiley, then-New York City Transit Authority President David Gunn, and then-Governor Mario Cuomo turned into a dramatization of the qualities that define work in the shop: the tension between insiders and outsiders, camaraderie and conflict, pride and accommodation, hostility and humor, and the games that workers and managers play at all levels as they establish authority and subordination.

⁗ I figured he's up in Albany and they eat pumpernickel up in Albany, and they don't have Italian pastries in Albany—you get great Italian pastries here. So I bought him some Italian pastries to have for breakfast and stuff. He came in his helicopter. And here we are, talking about the Italian pastries, and he's saying to Gunn and me, "I bet you these two guys from Boston can't name these pastries."

And I said, "Oh I think they can."

He says, "Oh, well, watch this, Mike."

And he says to David Gunn, "What's this thing here?" So he's pointing to what Italians call *ganol'*. It's spelled cannoli. And maybe in high-class Italian they say cannoli, but we always say, "Hey, ya got a *ganol'*?" you know.

So Gunn says, "That's a CAN-oh-lee." That's great.

So the governor started to laugh. And he's looking at me, and he says, "Ya hear him?"

So I says, "I heard him. He said it right."

"He said it right, are you crazy? He didn't say it right, he said 'CAN-oh-lee.'"

So I said, "Hey listen, governor, you're driving around, and these two guys are after my life. As far as I'm concerned, he said it right."

So he said, "Is that the kind of guy you are?"

I said, "You bet your life." (I'll never see that governor again.)

He hung around here for about an hour and a half, two hours. I showed him around, and he was good. We enjoyed him, we showed him all the important stuff.

I had an incident going on. I had a certain area where I was trying to get productivity out of this group of guys. And they said that they were going to make a lot of noise and disrupt this tour. They were dissatisfied that we were pushing for productivity. And I asked them not to do that.

"Don't bring embarrassment. We have a guest. We can fight when the guest isn't here. It isn't proper manners to be causing trouble when we have a guest. Show your manners, you guys, you know. You're all ready to cause a scene."

They said, "All right."

So we walked by that area, that little hotbed of labor dispute and labor tension, and they started to boo. "Booooo."

They're booing *me*, really. They're booing me, and they're booing him. And he says, "What's that all about?" So I don't want to get into this thing that I'm trying to get more productivity, so I told him that there's Republicans in every shop.

He was a great guy, the governor. They holler out, "Run for president, run for president."

So I said, "I think they're talking to me, governor."

He says, "They're not talking to you."

I didn't want to give him a helmet, because I said he was Barese. He came from Bari, Italy, and they don't need helmets—they got hard heads. So I said, "Governor, I don't think you need a helmet. You're a Barese."

So he says, "No, I'm Calabrese—give me the helmet."

But I had some fun, and I think the governor got a kick out of the fact that there was an Italian American kid who came from the bottom and worked his way up to the top. I think he got a kick out of that.

Plus he liked the place, and we had made a lot of

changes. And he was coming to see and talk about the changes that Kiley and Gunn put into place in terms of reorganizing the place and hiring supervisors and more managers. He came to see the results of those kinds of energies and plans. And he left satisfied, I think. IIIIII

CHAPTER 9

MATTERS OF COLOR

> I would say the Transit Authority is a city within the city. You have almost every type of person in the city employed in the Authority, from all nations of the world. And they jell, it's a good combination, it makes a good employment.
>
> *Emilio Robertino*, Superintendent of Building Facilities[1]

f the New York City transit workers had a dominant accent in the 1920s, it was Irish. So many Irishmen worked on the IRT that the line was nicknamed the "Irish Rapid Transit." In the 1990s, however, the dominant accent of the transit system is more likely to be that of Black America out of the South, the Caribbean, and the neighborhoods of New York City.

Today, some 66 percent of transit employees are minorities—Black, Hispanic, Asian or Indian. Of these minorities, almost 72 percent are African Americans. Although the Transit system is not yet completely integrated—African Americans and other people of color are still more likely to be in manual occupations than in administrative positions—they are spread through the transit workforce at a level unimaginable when the IRT opened at the beginning of this century. The integration of the transit workforce on a scale unmatched by most private businesses is one of the success stories of New York City—a benchmark in the long struggle for racial equality in the workplace.[2] And once in a while, it provides workers of all races and ethnic backgrounds a chance to discover common interests that transcend the color of their skin.

Like the city that surrounds it, the transit system is a patchwork of ethnic and racial groups. Within individual groups, cohesion can become exclusion. Fred McFarland recalls that when he first started work as a driver at private bus companies,

‖‖‖ These companies were owned by Irishmen and that's what they basically were. Italian, Black, forget it, Puerto Rican, forget it. But Italian—they had Italians come on this job but it took them a long time. This job at one time was basically, I'd say, 99 percent Irish.[3] ‖‖‖

Today, Italians are a standard presence in transit shops. When Penny Rohls went to work at the Bergen Street Shop, she recalls,

‖‖‖ It was largely Italian. And they would play opera music sometimes—walk into the shop and they were playing operas. It was crazy. And they cooked a lot, they did a lot of cooking. . . . They used to argue about who made the best tomato sauce—the gravy, they called it. Very competitive, these Italian guys, with their sauces.[4] ‖‖‖

In contrast, the African American entry into the transit work force was a protracted struggle. Thinking back to his childhood, Lionel Bostick recalls the fate of his playmate's father: he was gassed fighting for his country in World War I, but when he came home he was turned away when he sought work in Transit.[5] His story was typical. During the first four decades of the twentieth century, when African Americans looked for transit jobs—at first on either the private bus or subway companies and later on the city-owned IND line—a handful of them found cleaning work as porters. The rest had the door slammed in their faces.

The first effective challenge to such discrimination came from black workers, community groups, and civil rights organizations in the 1930s. In 1937, the integrated Transport Workers Union was recognized as the bargaining agent for workers on the IRT and BMT. Under the TWU, salary floors were set to benefit the poorest-paid workers. The policy meant better pay for African Americans, who were concentrated in the lowest paying jobs on the IRT and BMT. Nevertheless, the TWU, although uniquely integrated for its time, was a union with a white majority. Its leaders feared that their white members would oppose strenuous TWU efforts on behalf of black rights.[6]

Activists used the power of both the TWU and the city government to improve the lives of black transit workers. The first breakthrough came on the city-owned IND line. In 1934 Mayor Fiorello La Guardia, reminded by black activists that their votes in Harlem helped him win election, ordered that job assignments on the IND be made without regard to race. By the end of the decade, African Americans working on the IND had moved out of porter's positions and had found work as motormen, conductors, and clerks. In 1940, when the city took over the privately owned IRT and BMT, the National Association for the Advancement of Colored People convinced Mayor La Guardia to ban discrimination in the hiring of mechanics and motormen.[7]

The privately owned bus companies proved more resistant to change. But in March 1941, the TWU struck the bus companies for higher wages. In Harlem, black activists supported the union's cause. When the union won, the Harlem activists turned around and asked the TWU to support them in their fight for an end to racial discrimination in bus company hiring. At first the TWU was hesitant, but a community bus boycott—led by the charismatic preacher and activist Adam Clayton Powell, Jr.—defeated the companies in less than a month. In negotiations, the bus companies agreed to hiring quotas for

African Americans until their presence in the bus companies
matched their presence in the general population of Manhattan. This solution, complemented by the labor shortage of World
War II and state legislation passed in 1945 banning discrimination in most kinds of employment, including Transit, gave African Americans a solid and early start in their efforts to integrate
the transit workforce.[8]

Charles E. Smith, born in Atlanta, earned a B.A. in English
and moved to New York in 1930, where he found a place to
live at the YMCA.

> ⁣⁣⁣⁣ As I say, Adam Clayton Powell negotiated with the
> company, that since we were patrons of the bus and
> there were no Afro-American drivers, that they should
> have some. And that's the way it started. We were
> trained to operate the bus in the latter part of 1940, the
> first part of 1941. We completed that training, and then
> before we could go out in the passenger service, nego-
> tiations between Adam Clayton Powell and the com-
> pany broke down. . . . Approximately the latter part of
> January 1942, we were called again by Powell and the
> company and told that we would complete our training,
> which was in passenger service.[9] ⁣⁣⁣⁣

The first African American drivers all had high school or
college educations. Smith, a retired bus driver, recalls,

> ⁣⁣⁣⁣ Now here's the names of the original bus drivers
> that drove the bus February 11, 1942. The names were:
> Elmer O. Haney, Richard Farrell, Howe Arthur Lynn,
> Ed "Flash" Gordon [he was nicknamed "Flash" because
> he was an Olympic broad jump champ from the
> University of Iowa], Leon DeLowich, Vincent
> Cunningham, and Charles E. Smith. ⁣⁣⁣⁣

Smith recalls his days as one of the first black drivers.

> ⁣⁣⁣⁣ Naturally, it was a bit conspicuous, because every-
> one was watching you. It was a novelty, and naturally
> there were some derogatory remarks made over a

period of years after we first got on it. But as I say, I ignored them, I had a job to do. And as long as no one put their hands on me, whatever they say was just like water off a duck's back. ⅢⅢ

Despite this victory, discrimination stubbornly persisted. Thomas Granger, retired bus driver and a former personnel director, recalls looking for a job after World War II.

ⅢⅢ So I went up to the interview at 605 West 132nd Street, which was the personnel department of what was then the Fifth Avenue Coach Company. And the personnel department said, "Oh, Mr. Granger, come in. I talked to you several times over the phone." He was the vice president for administration or something. . . . I told him I'd like a job and he said, "What do you want to do?"

And I said, "Well, I'd like to work in your accounting department."

"Well, I'll be perfectly frank with you, Mr. Granger," he said. "Do you come from County Mayo or do you come from County Cork or do you come from any county in Ireland?"

I said, "What's that got to do with it?"

He said, "Well, Fifth Avenue Coach is a family affair, that is the administration part of it, the office, and if you're not from one of those counties, there's nothing I can do for you."

I said, "You mean to tell me, because of my background, my origins, that you can't give me a job?"

He said, "Well, I'm telling you, man to man, that if you go outside and try to make a fuss out of it, I'm going to deny I said it. We have no job openings for you."[10] ⅢⅢ

Black workers accustomed to discrimination could be reluctant to seek advancement. Marty Kaiser remembers one such case.

ⅢⅢ I'll tell you, we had at that time one black guy that

was a maintainer and one black guy that was a helper.
The guy I can remember very well, Bob, and he was
afraid to go up for the test for assistant foreman, and I
told him, "Why?"

He said, "Well, you know." At that time it wasn't
like it is now with black people getting ahead. He said,
"I'm colored, you know, and I come from down
South."

And I says, "So what's the difference? You're one of
us. You're a mechanic with us, and that's all that
counts."[11] ⦚⦚⦚⦚

Out of such conversations could emerge moments of friend-
ship, even solidarity, across racial lines. Assistant General Foreman Albert Schneider remembers.

⦚⦚⦚⦚ When I worked in the streetcar division there was
only one black man there and his name was Eddie
Davis. He worked in the electric department on a floor
about ten feet higher than the machine shop. He used
to come down to the bathroom and when he passed my
office he said to me, "Good morning, Brother
Schneider." And, honest to goodness, I felt so good. A
black man called me "Brother Schneider."[12] ⦚⦚⦚⦚

For Lloyd Tyler, an African American, the challenge was
fitting into a workplace where everyone seemed to congregate
with people who looked just like themselves.

⦚⦚⦚⦚ The old-time Irish guys in the main shop were
clannish, as well as the Italians were clannish and the
Jews that were working were clannish and the blacks
were clannish. I mean because everybody has their own
background. You know, a person that goes into a
neighborhood, if you moved into an Italian neighborhood and you are Jewish and there's four or five Jewish
people there you would feel comfortable there with
Jewish people. . . . But there was never anything that I
could say was outright racism. It might have been there
but it wasn't blatant.[13] ⦚⦚⦚⦚

Earnis Briant, a black foreman, found that some men resented working under him.

|||||| Fact of the matter, I was the first black mason foreman in the Transit. And the guys resented me but they didn't tell me this. I used to start into a room and I would hear them talking. One guy said to me, "I got more sick time than he got in the Transit Authority!" In other words, he got more sick leave that he accumulated for being here than I got time working in the Transit Authority. And a few other choice things.

So what I said was, "Well, maybe I don't go in there now. I'll go back in the locker room until they're finished talking. Then I'll go in there." But had I been the type of guy that burst in and said, "Ah, you're talking you so and so and so and so!" that would only ignite it. So by me turning around and going back in the office to let them talk it out, then I come in like nothing happened—it knocked the steam off a lot of stuff. . . . There's a time and a place for all things, and there's a time to drop it, to leave it where it is. And if you do that, usually you'll get along.[14] ||||||

Samuel Zelensky, a former senior trial lawyer for the Transit Authority, recalls a case where a passenger hurled racial insults at a black conductor.

|||||| There was a case where a passenger was on a train going to the Bronx, somewhere in the borough of the Bronx around Jackson Avenue Station, and I believe he had a few drinks under his belt. And the conductor was a black man. When the train reached a certain station he went over to him and said, "What's the big idea, you didn't keep the doors open?" and he abused him and called him various names, calling him "nigger" and so forth and so on.

Well, this conductor lost his head, and I don't blame him. He took a big plank of wood, and as the man who was calling him those names was already on the platform walking, he ran after him with this plank of wood and hit him over the head, as a result of which he received a fractured skull.

He did not die, but there was no question that the Transit Authority, through its agent the conductor here, was liable.

But I had to try the case. I put eight women on the jury, and I thought that women don't like anyone who calls names and they don't like anyone who starts a commotion or an argument with a conductor—they would not favor a litigant of that sort. And it worked like a charm, and they came in with a verdict for the defendant, on behalf of the Transit Authority.[15] |||||

Frances Murphy, office aide, remembers that her workplace friendships vastly expanded the range of people she knew.

||||| There's a lot of Italian people, a lot of Irish people, there's an awful lot of Polish people, there's all sorts of people, Chinese people. When I worked in revenue my first year here, I guess that was my most exciting year. I met people in revenue of every creed and denomination. We used to exchange recipes, we used to exchange stories. We sat together and they were great for bringing in coupons from the paper—put them down on that big table and you'd take what you want and you'd leave what you don't want. I met such nice people down there.

I never knew many Chinese people, I never knew many Indian people, and down there I met such lovely—I see them once or twice a week going out of the building, and it's almost ten years ago, and to me I'll never forget them because we had such great stories and exchanges and how they lived and how their children— I guess I was the oldest there, I had grandchildren, and now they're stopping to tell me about their new grandchildren and mine are all grown. It's a place where you could make friends and make ties and learn.[16] |||||

Emilio Robertino, in his rise from maintainer's helper to superintendent of building facilities, saw people of all races and nationalities find ways to get along.

ⅢⅢ I had a gang of men, I had some Puerto Rican fellas and I had a couple of colored fellas and a couple of white guys, and they would always stay within their groups. I have that today. You're not going to change that. I don't mean it's prejudiced, it's just that they feel more at ease with one another and the camaraderie is there. But I have a gang that's like a League of Nations—I have a Chinaman, I have a Russian, I have Italians, I have Irish. I have a couple of guys from the Islands and they're pretty happy. They seem to all get along. ⅢⅢ

CHAPTER 10

WORK, WOMEN, AND MEN

> Whoever is not used to seeing women around them
> all the time, they feel threatened by the women.
>
> *Elena Chang*, Lighting Maintainer[1]

The New York City Transit Authority employs some 44,310 people; 15 percent of them are women.

That doesn't mean that women are invisible in the world of transit. Although women are concentrated most heavily among office and clerical workers, where they are almost 47 percent of the workforce, they can be found everywhere in transit—from service maintenance to officials and administrators. Their presence throughout the transit workforce is part of the long-term growth in women's employment outside the home, an almost century-long trend that has transformed life in the United States.

In transit work, as in virtually every other American occupation, the arrival of women in a workplace traditionally dominated by men raises questions about everything from shop talk to the practice of considering some jobs "women's work" and some jobs "men's work." Add these issues to older discussions about how men and women balance family life and the demands of work in a twenty-four-hour transit system and you get a powerful dialogue about work, women, and men.

In their stories and conversations, transit workers explore what work means to them. Women and men talk about what happens when they work with one another: the pressure on women to prove themselves when they work in a dangerous and previously all-male environment like the tracks; the threatened feeling that comes over men when they see women doing a job, such as train operator, previously done only by men. They talk about balancing work and family life: what it means to a family when a father misses Christmas because he is working on a subway; what it means to a woman to be able to work nights and be with her children during the day. They figure out what it means to be a man or a woman, a parent or a spouse—and a transit worker.

Women are pushed into transit work by the same factors that send men into transit—everything from a desire for job security to a need to exercise their skills. Elena Chang, a secretary-turned-electrician, says, "I feel like a pair of pliers is my second set of hands."

Despite the dangers of electrocution and being run over by a train, Elena Chang found her first visit to the tracks "exciting."

> ⅢⅢ I liked it when the train came. When I didn't work for Transit I used to watch the train go by all the time. I used to be amazed at all the things people could do. And I'm still amazed at the big, big machines, the beauty of them, sometimes. People just look at them and say it's a piece of steel, but . . . ever since I came to Transit I started to ride the subway. And I don't take the subway for granted the way most people do. I admire the subway, I like the subway: big machines, big motors, big wheels, what makes them move. ⅢⅢ

For men who are used to seeing only other men at work, the arrival of women like Jenny Mandelino, structure main-

tainer, and Elena Chang forecasts profound changes. Shirley
Thaler, an associate staff analyst at the 240th Street Shop, recalls,

⫿⫿⫿ It's amazing what they think of us. This was really
their world for so long that it's very hard for them. As
hard as it was for us to adjust to this world, they had to
adjust to us being there.[2] ⫿⫿⫿

Part of the task of opening up jobs to women involves changing job titles so they will no longer presume that the worker is
a man. When "motorman" became "train operator," Theodore
Jones, a train operator, became angry. "We took the test to
become motormen. They changed it to train operator because
of the females. We resent that. We are motormen. They can
call the females anything else that they want to. But I want to
be called a motorman. Train operator weakens it."[3]

There are few women in the skilled crafts of transit, but
Joseph P. Fox, a senior railroad signal specialist, sees reasons for
them to seek such jobs.

⫿⫿⫿ I'm not a chauvinist. It's up to them. If they want
to do it, that's fine. It's not really what I would think is
a job that would really interest a gal, but the money is
good. And in considering some of these so-called
"women's jobs" where they don't pay and they're dead-
end, I think a woman would be silly not to come into
Transit where you can make a reasonably good salary
with avenues of advancement. The opportunity is here.
I wouldn't hesitate to have my daughter go in.[4] ⫿⫿⫿

Mike Lombardi sees women as a beneficial addition to the
Transit workforce.

⫿⫿⫿ Women brighten up the place. The place does
need women. It does. With women around, men act
better. When men are all together, they can be a pretty
rotten, raunchy bunch, sometimes.
I have five women in my household, between my
daughters, my wife, and my mother—I love women.

Women treated me wonderful all my life, I have
nothing against women.

But there are people here who hate women. They
really do. And it's for their dislike of women that they
don't want them here.

It's not because there's competition—they just dislike
women in general. They're people who've been
through divorces. They're wackos, there's a lot of
characters here.

But I would say women are welcomed by most
people, and treated with respect by most people.

Everybody knows that they're competent, everybody
knows that they kept this country going during the war
time, that women are capable of anything.[5]　||||||

Women tell more complicated stories. Penny Rohls, a superintendent, started out as a sign painter at the Bergen Street
Shop in Brooklyn.

||||||　I came to New York to go to art school at Pratt,
and ended up doing some at Pratt and actually graduat-
ing from Hunter College with a degree in English. I
thought I was going to teach at that point. But I always
missed the artwork, so I took courses in the evening
and became a textile designer. And then when my son
was born I stayed home with him for seven years, and
my husband thought it was time for me to go back to
work. . . .

And then a friend of a friend of a friend told me of a
job as a sign painter with the Transit Authority. And I
said, "Well, I don't do lettering, so I wouldn't possibly
qualify for a job as a sign painter."

And he said, "Well, no, you don't need to do that
because it's silkscreen work and it's just pasting down
letters." And the salary seemed pretty good. So I went
to the personnel department and I inquired about the
job, and they knew nothing about it.

So I went back to my friend who went back to her

friend who went back to his friend and said, "The job doesn't exist."

And he said, "Well, I know it does, I mean, I work at Bergen Street." So he met me at the Personnel Department and knew the job title and the location and the whole thing. (That was in '79.) And they began to laugh, and I said, "What's so funny about this? It's a job for a sign painter."

So finally one of them said, "But they don't have facilities for women at Bergen Street, so why would she want to work there?"

So now—of course this is the days of ERA and everything—now my ears are beginning to pick up and you know, "What's wrong?"

So they made a few phone calls and they found out that the supervisor at Bergen Street was willing to share his bathroom with me, so I wouldn't have to go into the men's locker room. I would have a bathroom. So then the person that had brought me there said, "Well, maybe you ought to just come out and look around and see what it looks like. It's like a fortress out there."

So we went out on the train, and we walked in the front door, and I said, "Uh, huh!" Now I see why they were laughing. Because there were no women at Bergen Street. I don't know, there were maybe a hundred and fifty guys and NO women. And it was really a novelty. But they were very, very sweet. So my husband said, "Well, try it for two weeks. If you don't like it, you can buy yourself a new dishwasher and quit."

So that was how I started. It was just going to be "we'll-see-for-two-weeks."[6] ⅢⅢ

After she was settled in at her job, she heard about the preparations for her arrival.

ⅢⅢ   Management went in with a bullhorn on a Friday before I was going to start on a Monday, and ordered

the guys to take down their pinups, and that they
would not use four-letter words, and they would be
gentlemen. And the guys were infuriated to be talked to
like children. So when I arrived on Monday, they were
a little hostile. They were also very curious so they
came around to talk. At the end of the first week I felt
that I was accepted—to a degree. And they were very
candid. They told me in no uncertain terms, "Whatever
you do is your concern, but if you were MY wife or
daughter, you would not be in this plant."

And it was kind of like being treated a little bit like a
mascot. Sometimes they were overly protective. I got
very tired about having them apologize for cursing.   ⅢⅢ

Jenny Mandelino, who learned carpentry from her uncle as
a child, told her fellow carpenters in Transit, "Act like your-
selves. I've been in this field all my life, so I know exactly what
goes on. Don't watch every word you're saying. Just don't direct it at me."

But she took direct action on the pinups. "One of the guys
went on vacation—he had pictures of girls all over his desk.
When he came back, they were changed to guys. I changed
them all to guys. It eased the tension. It was fun. It was something to do."[7]

Diane Leibovitz, a deputy superintendent at the 240th Street
Shop, learned the value of women's work on a kibbutz in Israel, where women are as eligible for important jobs as men.
She came to the Transit Authority after years of work in city
government.

ⅢⅢ   The gossip was that somebody was going to rape
me in a shop at night and then it would ruin it for
everybody and everybody would get into trouble. That
was supposedly a major fear. That I wouldn't be able to
handle myself. The other fear, I think, was that I'd be a
spy for management and tell all their secrets to everybody. The "legitimate concern" was that I didn't have
technical background and that I wouldn't understand

what was going on, that I wouldn't be able to
learn.[8] ⫶

Leibovitz lacked the mechanical background of some transit
officials, but in her view she compensated for it with managerial experience from her service in city government. She decided that she first had to learn the culture of the shop.

⫶ I did things that they evidently thought I should be
able to do and didn't expect me to do. Like making
myself part of the workplace. Climbing around trains,
not being afraid to get dirty, not being afraid to handle
employees, going out and talking to people, doing what
I considered my job. They didn't expect me to know
that that's what I was supposed to do but I knew
that. ⫶

Leibovitz recalls that a lot of shop life involved cursing and
shop talk, some of it meant to insult. She learned to play the
game and give it back.

⫶ What was hard for me was to not give it back in
ways that would embarrass them. Because you have to
be aware of that also. They think they're big shots. It's
easy to embarrass men if you want to.

They tease me about everything. They tease me
about how I dress, and how and if my hair is curly one
day or not curly one day or if I'm not wearing lipstick.
So I just tease back that's all. It's harmless, it's all meant
in good jest. It's just general, the skirt's too tight or the
pants are or you're gaining weight again.

You know, they are all terribly concerned about
how much they weigh. All the men are. They're
terribly concerned about whether they're getting fat or
thin or whether they can still tie their shoelaces but
nobody ever said anything to me about whether I was
fat or thin.

Except today I got told that my rear was getting
larger. I said, "No it's not."

But the fact that they can say that to me like they say it to each other means that I'm part of the group and I take it that way. I don't assume that it's an insult. ⫴

Elena Chang's experiences with men on the job were different. Even though most of her friends outside work are men, she enjoyed no special advantages in dealing with men on the job. Life at work was an ongoing contest for her.

⫴ Most of the electricians are welcoming me to work with them. But some of them are real chauvinist and they don't like women around where they work. . . . I don't participate in their conversation. I don't like them degrading the female. But there's nothing I can do. I'm not going to start arguing with them, I'm not going to start asking them to respect me, otherwise they will do it in spite. ⫴

Chang says everyone notices that there are no other women around and makes cracks about it.

⫴ But I have a smart mouth. I answer back. Depends on what they say. Sometimes when they pour cement on the tracks we provide electricity for the coffee, and we make sure that the coffeemakers are working. If I see somebody out of our gang taking a cup of coffee he says to me, "Can I take a cup of coffee?" The reason why he's asking me is because he wants to talk to me. So I say to him, "You have to pay for it."

He says to me, "If I pay for it, you must reach down my pocket."

And that doesn't faze me. I don't care, I'll reach down his pocket and when I'm about to reach, he will go away.

Somebody had a nutcracker. So he said to me, "I'm going to crack your nuts."

So I took it away from him and I said, "I'll crack *your* nuts."

. . . And ever since, he hasn't bothered me at all. ⫴

New York City Transit is a twenty-four-hour system with a ceaseless demand for labor. Some parents like that because it makes it easier to set up child care. Brenda Hayes, a general superintendent, notes,

IIIII There are a lot of females that like to work during the night. Because if you have someone to monitor the kids once you put them in bed, by the time they are up, you are finished working, you're home again. So you have all day. And if they're in school or if they're in day care or whatever, when they come out then that's when you're able to do all of the things with them.[9] IIIII

For other transit workers, an around-the-clock job puts a strain on a marriage. For husbands and wives, the problems can be profound. Jeffrey Van Clief recalls,

IIIII I spend days here without going home. Without seeing my people. My wife at one time considered herself a "transit widow." She said, "I don't see you. You're married to the job, you're not married to me."

That's one of the biggest things that I found working here. You really got to have a woman who's dedicated to you and your job. . . . Guys in cars and shops who work in barns and main shops, they got it easy. They have a steady job, eight to four, Saturday and Sunday off. But you got guys like road car inspectors, track and structure, motormen and conductors, they don't get Saturday and Sunday off. They don't get summer vacation, they get winter vacations.

I don't know about today but years ago that's the way it was with me when I first started working here. Marriage—you had to have a good wife. A lot of women today get fed up, you got a big divorce rate here. . . .

And my wife hated this job with a passion. Last year they had a dinner for anybody twenty-five years in this place. Now, I got thirty-two and they invite me to the twenty-five-year dinner. I tell my wife, "Look, you got to go with me to the twenty-five-year dinner."

"No, this job stinks, I don't like it, I never see you, you didn't raise your kids up, you was always working, and now they want to honor you," this and that.

I said, "You're my wife. You got to go."

Very reluctant, very reluctant. Didn't want to go. . . . I made her go. She fought me in the car, argued in the car about my crazy TA friends and all this nonsense, you know. . . . She's in the car and she's driving me nuts all the way to this place.

And we get upstairs, and the elevator doors open. Who's standing there but Mr. Gunn? [David Gunn, then president of the Transit Authority.] And he pins a corsage on her. He catered to her and she was so exuberant. They gave her roses. The pin that I got, the twenty-five-year pin, I gave it to her. They just catered to her. . . . And, man, she was in her glory.[10] ▥

The next week, Van Clief was invited to a dinner for workers with thirty years in the system. He asked his wife and she said she would go.

▥   Then finally she says, "You know, I shouldn't complain. You educated your son. You bought me a home. You're going to retire on a good pension one day. I shouldn't complain. But that's a hard thirty-something years we've been married." . . .

She says it was a hard life. She says it's like a sailor on a ship leaving a wife home. She says, "Many a Christmas Eve I cried because you wasn't in the house, you're working. A normal family, my family everybody got together and says, 'Where's your husband?' He's working."

With summer vacation, your kid's out for the summer and you got winter vacations. . . . Now we're getting a summer vacation so I take care of my grandchildren and my son is jealous. . . .

I said, "I took care of you in a different way. As a father I couldn't take you fishing. Once in a blue moon. Couldn't take you to sports games because I was never home. You had a roof over your head. You had clothing. You had money in your pocket. I didn't run away from you. I didn't leave you. I was there. But I was there the wrong time. I didn't have Saturdays and Sundays off, I had Mondays and Tuesdays or Thursdays and Fridays. So, it wasn't that I was neglecting you because I couldn't help myself. . . . It's my living. It's what I know best. It's something that it was an opportunity for me and I took advantage of the opportunity. This is my life. I dedicated myself to this. I'm sorry that you felt that way, but you're here. You're enjoying the fruits so it can't be that bad."

The divorce rate here is very bad. I find that you talk to a lot of guys here, you really get personal with them, you find out that this is the second wife. Other guys I know married girls from the TA. Someone who understands, someone who knows how he's working, someone that understands. A lot of people don't understand. IIIIII

CHAPTER 11

UNION TALK

I believe in unions as being for the employee,
and the unions have come a long way. They've
gotten a lot of things done for the employee that
might not have been done had they not been there.
And it's a way of bringing the employees together
into a unified unit. Into a brotherhood, where they
work for the benefit of each other.

Stanley Stern, Dispatcher[1]

They worked twelve hours a day, seven days a week for
wages that hovered just above the poverty line. Their
backs were bent from stooping and their hands were
curled from holding wrenches. The men who drove buses got
ulcers so often that the ailment was called "driver's stomach."
They faced three-day suspensions for unauthorized cigarette
breaks. So little time was allowed for toilet breaks that in 1935,
one IRT conductor was killed as he rushed across the subway
tracks trying to relieve himself without putting his train behind
schedule. Such were the lives of transit workers for the first
three decades of the twentieth century, before the improvements

in working conditions won by Local 100 of the Transport Workers Union. The union gained the right to represent workers on the IRT and BMT lines in 1937 and later became representative of workers on the IND.[2]

Six decades later, the TWU and Local 100 face many of the problems that bedevil the American labor movement: threats of downsizing, leadership that finds it difficult to inspire the membership or capture the sympathy of the public, and internal disagreements.[3] Nevertheless, the TWU and Local 100 deserve credit for being the instrument that transit workers used to transform their lives and their labor in New York City. At its best, the story of Local 100 is a story of solidarity and courage in pursuit of a common good.

Local 100, which represents all hourly employees, is the largest of the unions that represent transit workers. And in the history of the Transport Workers Union and Local 100, no one looms larger than the shrewd, fiery, funny, and charismatic Michael J. Quill. Quill helped to organize the TWU in 1934 and was elected its president the following year; he later held a seat on the New York City Council and served as a vice president of the Congress of Industrial Organizations.

Born in Ireland, Quill fought in the Irish Republican Army, then immigrated to New York in 1926 and went to work on the subway. He found a heavily Irish workforce. He also found men driven by memories of poverty in Ireland and later the desperation of the Great Depression working long and irregular hours in dirty and difficult conditions.

Much of the misery of pre-union transit work was rooted in hard economics. By the 1930s the New York City mass transit industry, with its tangled web of public financing, private management, and intricate investment, was plagued by shortages of capital, aging equipment, and high fixed costs. Subway fares were legally set, with wide public support. As costs rose, the transit companies could not raise their fares. To save money, they scrimped on salaries and safety, as Marty Kaiser, general superintendent in charge of structures, relates.

ⅢⅢ   When I first started here, most of the men were

from the old IRT, and in those days, equipment was
expensive and men were cheap. So they really didn't
care if a man got hurt or not. . . . They would say to a
guy, two men, "Pick up that stick." When they said "a
stick," a stick was a twelve-by-twelve beam twenty-foot
long, and the thing weighed a ton. But they didn't care
if the man got hurt. They just got another guy off the
boat from Ireland and they'd put him to work and they
didn't care.[4] ⸾⸾⸾⸾⸾

Tim Griffin, who went to work on the BMT in 1930, recalls
his first seven years on the job, before the union came in, as
"seven years of hell."

⸾⸾⸾⸾⸾ You'd come in at four o'clock in the morning.
That would be the first report. And you wouldn't get
any work. You'd sit around there maybe till three or
four o'clock in the afternoon. You'd be lucky if you
got a day or two days work a week.

You had no regular set hours. Sometimes I wouldn't
come home till half past three in the morning and I'd
have to come in again at five o'clock for report. Sometimes I'd sit in the depot. Come home. Go to sleep. Get
up. Go to work.

I put in some brutal hours. . . . It used to just about
pay my board.[5] ⸾⸾⸾⸾⸾

John O'Brien recalls, "The idea of an eight- or nine-hour
day wasn't known. There were nine-and-a-half-, ten-, and
twelve-hour runs."

⸾⸾⸾⸾⸾ Days off were unknown. . . . For us coming from
holy, saintly Ireland and not getting church on Sunday,
it was a sort of slap in the puss. I suppose we had to eat
and in order to eat we had to work, so we had little
choice in the matter, and work we went to and forgot
about the church. You might get a Sunday off if you
told them your aunt's uncle was dead or your third or
fourth cousin or something like this but that was the
only way you'd get a day off.[6] ⸾⸾⸾⸾⸾

In the Transport Workers Union organizing drive, union men and allied organizers from the Communist Party faced company spies. TWU supporters wore their union buttons on the inside of their coat collars and spoke in a secret code: "Did you see the light?" meant "Did you join the union?" An answer of "yes" meant that a man could be trusted.[7]

Griffin recalls a story about a fellow worker named Johnny Regan, who hid his union button until the day after Local 100 was voted in. His boss called him in to his office.

ⅢⅢ "Johnny Regan, I can understand some of these young hotheads joining the union, but I'm amazed that a long-headed fellow like yourself ever let Mike Quill talk you into this Communist union."

"Mr. Johnson," he said, "Mike Quill [or] any other Mike couldn't talk me into anything I didn't want to join. But Mr. Johnson, you and the rest of the bosses, the way they treated the men, they were the best organizers on the property." ⅢⅢ

Quill, who helped found the Transport Workers Union in 1934, went on to become its most memorable leader. His nickname was "Red Mike," and from 1934 to 1948, he worked closely with the Communist Party, then a strong force in a labor movement faced with the challenge of the Great Depression. Most transit workers were not communists, but they accepted Quill's politics because he brought improvements in working conditions. Among Irish workers, who were numerous in transit, he also had a good reputation as an Irish Republican.

Victor De Santo recalls that the old IRT men held Mike Quill in the highest regard because he got them out of the "hell-holes" of the pre-union era in Transit.

ⅢⅢ They worshipped Mike Quill because he took them out of a dungeon. . . . They were always striking, they had no union to back them up. Then when Mike Quill came up here they seemed to get better working conditions and everything else that goes with it. They actually did worship him. .... Mike Quill was God to them.[8] ⅢⅢⅢ

Of course, Quill did not change the lives of transit workers all by himself. His success was possible only because of the organizing of scores of transit workers whose names have not entered the history books, like Mike Lombardi's father.

> ⅢⅢⅢ My father was with Mike Quill. Quill used to come to my house. I loved Quill.
> I used to go to all the TWU meetings. I sat right in the front row. I used to watch the Susskinds and all these people interview Mike Quill, and how he used to cut them up into bait. I used to watch *Meet the Press* in the morning when they'd have four geniuses interviewing him, and how he would just cut them up one at a time. I used to love it. I was eighteen at the time. He used to come to the house.
> My father helped organize the TWU. Because at the time it needed to be organized. Management brought it upon themselves. They gave them lousy raises or they didn't give them raises. They gave them Christmas, all the holidays off, but they forgot to pay them. There was a lot of reasons for the union. The union existed because they weren't treated properly: The city complained how strong the union was, but if it wasn't for the mishandling of their workers, they wouldn't have had a union.[9] ⅢⅢⅢ

Quill, for all his fighting spirit and repeated threats of a subway strike, led only one massive strike in New York City. Having won only modest gains in wages for his members since the 1950s, Quill called a strike that began January 1, 1966. When a judge ordered him to lead the union back to work, Quill said he could "drop dead in his black robes." TWU leaders, including Quill, were imprisoned for contempt of court.

Lombardi walked picket lines in the 1966 strike.

> ⅢⅢⅢ It was freezing. I was going on to picket duty at 207th Street and I remember picking up some people

who were waiting for a bus that was never going to come. And I got them in my car, and I didn't tell them that I worked for the Transit Authority. Most of them were sympathetic, even though it was vicious weather and stuff, they were sympathetic. They were saying both sides have to be heard. They had a lot of common sense, these people. They didn't know where I worked, but there was one particular guy who had absolutely no use for transit workers. I threw him out. I went a couple of blocks, I said, "You, out." He didn't know why. Then I told the guy that, "Yes, I work for the Transit Authority." He had absolutely no use for us.   ⫿⫿

Joseph Allotta was on a picket line at Stillwell Avenue. He was excited, but he was taken aback when he saw scabs going in.

⫿⫿   And you would say to yourself, "How could they?" They say, "Well, I got a family." Everybody in that line had a family. But it made me feel good to go out, because I figured it's for something that we're fighting for. The only thing I hated was that everybody had to get hurt. The whole city had to get hurt because nobody could get to work.[10]   ⫿⫿

The 1966 strike, which brought considerable hardship to the city and considerable criticism to the union, lasted twelve days. The final settlement, which very much favored the TWU, was Quill's last achievement. He died soon afterward and was mourned at Saint Patrick's Cathedral, his coffin covered with an IRA flag.[11]

Local 100 of the TWU has staged only one other citywide strike, a 1980 walkout under the leadership of John Lawe that was principally over wages, pensions, and benefits. Mayor Ed Koch used his considerable talents for public relations to rally sentiment against the strike, which ended after eleven days under pressure from a contempt of court citation.[12]

The strike exposed rifts between older members of the union, who were mostly Irish, and a growing number of younger African Americans and Latinos, who demanded greater representation in the union and tougher stands against management.[13] The racial and ethnic divisions were a reprise of splits in earlier generations of transit workers. Mike Lombardi points out that it was once hard for an Italian to see a future in a union dominated by Irishmen. "I really did want to become a union leader," he recalls. "It was like my ambition."

> ⅢⅢ Most of the leaders were Irish from Ireland. There wasn't any room for an Italian. There wasn't room for a Puerto Rican. There wasn't a token black, a token Puerto Rican, a token Italian. I saw the handwriting on the wall.
>
> My father even advised me. He used to write for the *TWU Express*. He told me, "At this time, it's no good. You won't catch a break there. You're better off in the civil service system taking tests where people don't care who you are." And he was right. To make it in the union, it would have to be who you knew, how hard you worked, and what connections you had. People tend to want to be with people that they're comfortable with. I'm sure if it was an Italian union, there would be no room for the Irish. I'm not saying that they're just prejudiced; I'm just saying that people tend to want to be with the people that they're comfortable with, that they share customs and cultures and music and whatever. ⅢⅢ

Today, of the 44,310 people in the Transit workforce, 29,393—or 66 percent—are African Americans, Latinos, Asians, or Native Americans. African Americans account for almost 72 percent of Transit's "minorities."[14] In 1998 the president of Local 100 is Willie James, an African American. (His predecessor was Damaso Seda, a Latino.) District Council 37, whose locals represent more than a thousand transit workers—mostly in clerical positions—is led by an African American, Stanley Hill.

A dissident group within Local 100, New Directions, argues that union leadership should be more open with its members and take tougher stands against management on issues such as wages, benefits, and the use of private contractors to perform jobs that would otherwise be done by transit workers. Members of New Directions, who came close to winning control of the union in a 1994 election, have charged that they are singled out for disciplinary actions—an allegation which transit officials reject. In 1997 and 1998, they again came close to winning control of the local in hard-fought elections that pit the incumbent Willie James against a challenger from New Directions, Tim Schermerhorn, who is also an African American.[15]

Since the 1980 strike, members of Local 100 have disagreed with management over issues such as wages, downsizing, work rules (such as whether trains should be run without conductors), health care benefits, safety conditions, and parental leave. Subcontracting of work that would otherwise be done by transit workers in Local 100 has also been a point of contention. There has been talk of strikes within the union, but the militancy of transit workers can be uneven. In voting on the 1996 contract, for example, subway workers faced with the prospect of layoffs were most hostile to the contract; bus drivers, whose circumstances were different, supported it.[16]

In 1996 the MTA and Local 100 clashed over a proposal to use welfare recipients to clean the subways. Management, strapped by cuts in city and state aid, saw this as a way to reduce costs; the union saw it as a move to eliminate the jobs of its members. At the height of the disagreement the MTA threatened to lay off as many as two thousand workers and replace them with a cleaning company. Eventually the two sides reached an agreement: up to five hundred cleaning jobs would be eliminated through attrition and thousands of welfare recipients would be brought in to clean buses and subways. In return, no union workers would be laid off through 1999. However, the agreement was stymied because the city refused to supply the welfare recipients to MTA/New York City Transit: Mayor Rudolph Giuliani would not allow welfare recipients to take jobs that were previously done by paid workers.[17]

There are probably as many opinions on Local 100 as there are members. Vincent Ricciardelli rejects the belief that the union has allowed workers to become lazy.

⁞⁞⁞⁞⁞ We didn't nitpick—I mean, the image that's out there is that the union would protect goldbrickers. And that wasn't the case. Sometimes it did happen, I'm not going to say it didn't. Sometimes it did but the group that I was in, we were told right from the first day that you got to do the job. You know, if you get your butt in hot water and the job is done we can work, we can try and make a deal. But if you're not doing the job properly and you go and get yourself in trouble—and this was the union people said this—forget it, you're dead meat. So we were kind of taught when we first came in that there was importance to doing the job, doing it correctly. And there was quality work being put out at that time, contrary to what some people have made public.[18] ⁞⁞⁞⁞⁞

Whitfield Lee says management should recognize workers' human needs and act appropriately.

⁞⁞⁞⁞⁞ Management has one way of thinking, and the union has another way of thinking. And I guess somewhere in there you have to find a balance. Management has to understand that you're dealing with people, and when you're dealing with people, you're dealing with human nature. And when you're dealing with human nature, everybody's not going to react the same or do the same. . . . But you can get a lot done by giving a guy a pat on the back and saying, "Nice job!" once in a while, other than coming down on him all the time. . . .

I'd be the first to admit that you need supervision in any body of men because they have to have management supervision. But they need a course in dealing with people today. You just don't jump all over a person till you know what the reason for this person's acting this way. Because he might have a reason, especially if the man or woman has been doing that job all the time.[19] ▫

Local 100 is not as prominent a force in New York City as it was in the days of Mike Quill.[20] It is still, however, an important presence in the world of transit. "I was interested in seeing a strong union," says Lionel Bostick, an African American and a former railroad clerk, "because I always felt that an employer never gave an employee anything out of the goodness of his heart. He gave what he had to give."[21]

CHAPTER 12

MOVING INTO MANAGEMENT

In supervision, you're like a father confessor, you're a mother, a father, you don't realize what the title comes with, but you are.

Emilio Robertino, Superintendent of Building Facilities[1]

To a degree that is ever more rare in the American workplace, transit workers can start out in low-level manual positions and, by passing civil service tests and accumulating seniority, become supervisory and managerial personnel.

The process is neither easy nor automatic, and recent efforts to hire personnel directly into management have cut off some opportunities to rise from the ranks. Nevertheless, at the top levels of the transit system it is possible to meet managers who have climbed from very ordinary jobs to positions of unusual authority. Different managers learn different lessons from the experience: some embrace the hierarchy and the opportunities for command that go with it; others maintain a sympathy for people who have to receive orders.

Richard Oakes takes great pride in his advancement through the transit system.

‖‖‖ There's places to go here. You can move ahead. I can remember back when I was a maintainer, and we were discussing, someday maybe you'd like to be a foreman, and we were talking maintainers amongst themselves—never dreaming that I was going to not only be a foreman, be an assistant supervisor, now a deputy superintendent. I don't know, I may even go higher before I retire. It only seems like yesterday that I came here. But this is a good job. I sincerely believe that.[2] ‖‖‖

Oakes's first dreams were of something other than a career in Transit, but the job grew to satisfy him anyway. "I wanted to be in the merchant marine, or in the navy, captain of my own ship," he says. "But that never came to be, so . . . this is my ship today."

More common, however, are workers who make a place for themselves in the system without climbing to the very top. Some remain hourly employees because they are afraid that civil service tests will reveal weaknesses in their writing and work skills. Some like the hours or the location of a job and seek no further.

Whitfield Lee, a railroad clerk, considered trying to become a supervisor and then thought twice.

‖‖‖ Those jobs are usually stressful, and a few thousand dollars more to me, it's not worth the stress. . . . Being a clerk is a different kind of stress because you're dealing on a one-to-one basis with your customers. In supervision and management, you're answering to a lot of people. It's a stressful job.[3] ‖‖‖

Joseph Allotta, a cleaner, considered what moving up in Transit would mean to him.

‖‖‖ A lot of people said, "Why didn't you get advanced? Why didn't you go ahead?"

The only promotion we had at the time I came on is to railroad clerk, which I wouldn't take. To me, I think it is the second worst job in the whole system—next to a bus driver—because first of all, you're confined into that booth. A railroad clerk, if they need a comfort relief, they either have to get a cleaner or they have to call the office. Now what if you're in a bind where you have to go right away? That's number one.

Number two, I have a little claustrophobia. I don't like to be closed in where I can't get out for any length of time if it's possible. Then, all that responsibility—for what? At the time it was ten cents an hour different. The responsibility, if there is any money missing, you had to pay for it. Everything—you're responsible for everything that's in that booth. Once you're relieved, if a flashlight's missing, you had to pay for it. . . . ⅢⅢ

Allotta considered trying for a promotion to conductor, and then realized it would mean giving up cleaner's work routines he had come to value.

ⅢⅢ I decided to stay, and now I'm not sorry a bit. Because as a cleaner, you have a little more freedom. You know what I'm saying? If I have to go to the toilet, I don't have to depend on anybody. If I need a cup of coffee, I don't have to depend on them. I go downstairs, I get a cup of coffee. Any of these things you need, I have that freedom that I didn't have before. And like I said, I wasn't sorry after that. Like I said, if you do your job, your boss doesn't bother you, you're like your own boss. And this is why I stood the way I did.[4] ⅢⅢ

For workers who decide to become managers, the choices include going to work on the staff of their union or moving up in Transit through the civil service. If they climb the civil service ladder, they move from labor to management—and change perspectives, as Marty Kaiser recalls.

ⅢⅢ One of the fellas I was a maintainer with was a

foreman and I was an assistant supervisor at nights, and he had a job to do—track drains. I told him he had to get it done, and take out whatever tools it was and make sure you sign for them. And he refused to sign for it.

I told him, "Hey, if you don't do it, I'm going to bring you up on charges, get you broken back down to maintainer." And for a while there, he didn't talk to me, but then afterwards he started realizing I've got my job to do. . . . And now we're very good friends. He's retired now, in fact his son works here now, and we're very good friends.

And the same thing happened a few times at nights, with the people I worked with as hourly people. They became foremen and I had moved up ahead of them to assistant supervisor. I had run-ins with them, but my job is my job, I work for the TA, and that's it. I'm going to do the best I can for the Transit Authority. Plain and simple.

When I was assistant supervisor at nights, we had a snow emergency, and in an emergency, people come first. We had to get the trains moving, and I told everybody, "Nobody goes home, you must work." Two of the men said, "We don't care, we're going home." For that there I gave them three days off in the street without pay. Two men. Two men who are good friends now. Not that they come to my house or anything, but both of them are foremen now. This is twelve years later. They're very happy, I'm very happy with them. They still talk about it: "You know what you gave me?" and I tell them, "Right." They say, "Well, we understand it."[5] |||||

Thomas Granger, who began his career in Transit as a bus driver, found it "very strange" to go from labor to management.

||||| But I felt it gave me a better advantage because I understood some of the problems that the drivers had out there, and I knew that a lot of their complaints

were legitimate. And then when they would come and tell me—after I was able to interview and had the say-so I was supposed to when I first went in the job—when they come in and tried to jive me about what they were doing, I said, "You can't fool me, man, I know what it's all about, because I had been out there in it myself." I said, "Don't give me that crap."[6] ⅢⅢ

Mike Lombardi, once a shop steward in the TWU, concluded that as an Italian American he didn't have much chance of advancement in an Irish-dominated union. So he made a switch.

ⅢⅢ So anyways—now I'm 100 percent management. Once I got into supervision I jumped over the fence, you know, don't get me wrong. I play for the team that I'm on. . . . I love the people I work with, and I treat them with respect and dignity. I do—I mean, I try. So that's where I get that from. I get it from the compassionate home. I was 100 percent union.[7] ⅢⅢ

Former manual workers who move up to management sometimes miss the days when they worked with their hands. "Yeah, every once in a while I go downstairs in the shop and piddle around with the guys on something, do a little physical work," says Emilio Robertino, a maintainer's helper who worked his way up to being superintendent of building facilities. "Guys frown upon it: 'What, you're the boss, you're doing our work.'" But Robertino likes to show them that he still has his skills.

As the Transit Authority increases the number of managers from outside its ranks, new managers come in who did not work their way up like the old-timers. A clash of perspectives results, as Carol Meltzer observes.

ⅢⅢ I think that what happens is that a lot of people that do come in horizontally don't understand that experience is very, very important and they . . . discount the importance of it . . . and that's something that I never did. You know, if somebody had twenty years as a clerk

or twenty years as a cleaner I would listen to them. Or
even five years, or even a year. I mean, that type of
experience is so critical. And if you're going to come in
straight out of college and think you know everything—and some people do—it's a big mistake because
obviously the people that are here are going to have a
problem with it and you certainly can't blame them
because they have come through the school of hard
knocks.[8]   IIIII

To Emilio Robertino, the best way to learn the transit system is from the inside out and from the bottom up.

IIIII   I don't think that people from the outside have the
feel for it. . . . Like I came up for many years, and my
experience they'll never get, they'll never get what I
learned. They can learn it, but they will never get the
experience of all of it. They can learn where Forty-
second Street and Eighth Avenue is, know what the
station looks like, but they're not going to learn the
other things, the little parts of that station that I knew
from working in that area.

Like we had a water main break, I was working
nights at the time, I had a leak gang. We had a water
main break on Broadway, which is two good full
blocks away from Forty-second Street and Eighth
Avenue. Now if you're familiar with the station,
there's a lower level to that station. Well, the water
was up to the ceiling in the lower level. . . . This was
at night, so there were no trains and no people down
there.

Well, we went down there with the pump car, we
had to pump that station out. We realized that as the
water was going down, there was a residue of mud on
the walls and nobody believed how high the water was
until they looked at that mud line. And it's little things
like that, that guy wouldn't know, that there was water
up to the ceiling at that particular station, unless he was

there. He probably still could never visualize the magnitude of the water that was in that area. ⅢⅢ

Over the course of his career in transit, Joseph Fox moved from being a maintainer to being senior railroad signal specialist. "When I shifted, I went from just reacting into designing. I had something to say about how the system worked. I thought that was rewarding. I could to a degree control how the system worked, which was important."[9]

When Stanley Stern became a dispatcher he got to use more of his talents for organization and management. Moving into labor relations, he feels "a reward" for helping transit workers straighten out their lives.

> ⅢⅢ One conductor who was really on the brink of being dismissed, and his violations were so outstanding—they were really bad. We came very, very close to filing for dismissal. And when I sat in the hearing room, he literally broke down and cried, and I gave him a chance to recover, and I asked him, "What is your problem?"
>
> He said, "I've been having problems with my wife, and my daughter ran away from home. I started drinking."
>
> So I said, "Don't tell me about the drinking. I don't want to hear about it, because I have to do certain things in certain ways. If you tell me about your drinking, I'm going to have to suspend you now and send you for counseling. As for that, you take it up with the union and the EAP [Employee Assistance Program]. But as far as the other things are concerned, you can't let that affect your job, even though it will affect your job. I don't feel I'm going to file for dismissal just yet. Go for counseling. Take a leave of absence. Get yourself straightened out. Get your daughter into counseling."
>
> I gave him a couple of telephone numbers, people to call in the Employee Assistance Program. I said, "Get yourself straightened out." I said, "Come back in three months and tell me what position you're in."

In three months he called me and said, "I can't come in right now. I'm upstate New York, and I'm getting myself dried out. My wife is going to counseling, and my daughter is back in school, and she's straightened herself out. We got her into counseling and all that. I'll call you when I come home, back to the city."

I said, "Fine."

He came down about two months after that and he walked in, and he was all smiles and happy and all that. And he said, "I'm back to work. My daughter's engaged. My wife is working. We have a terrific family, and I've got a grandchild on the way. And all I can tell you is thanks." He said, "I owe you."

I said, "No, you don't owe me anything. You owe yourself. It's more than that, you owe the job and your family. So keep it up." . . . I literally helped to save a man's life. And it felt good.[10] ‖‖‖

Still, moving into management also has its burdens. Mike Lombardi recognizes them.

‖‖‖ You know, what I miss working with the hands is that I didn't have any problems when I worked with my hands. When you left the job at four o'clock, you left the job. There's no way I can leave this job—the job's always with me. So there's that burden of pressure that while you're away, all those trains—and I am responsible for about 365 trains a day, you know, each train has eight or ten cars on it—anything happens to one of those trains because of poor maintenance, they injure somebody or—that's on *my* conscience. That's pressure, and you're constantly exposed to things that could be terrible, catastrophic. And some of these things you don't have control over, some things you do. There's constant pressure.

When I was a maintainer I was carefree and unburdened—I miss that. I do miss that. ‖‖‖

Brenda Hayes, who moved from being a railroad clerk to

general superintendent of the Station Department Command
Center, misses having the ability to plan her day.

⫿⫿⫿ Very few supervisors work eight hours. Because
once in a while your night is going really good and
seven o'clock in the morning—which is an hour before
you are supposed to get off—there's a problem. Or
there's a derailment. Or there's a disruption or you have
a clerk that's sick and you must take them to the
hospital and then there goes your whole night, you see.
. . . One of the things that we always say when we
become a supervisor is that you cannot plan your
day.[11] ⫿⫿⫿

Jeffrey Van Clief found that communication and a human
touch are important tools for a manager.

⫿⫿⫿ If you really want to accomplish things here and
you're really enthusiastic and you get uptight you're not
going to go nowhere. You are going to get yourself sick
and get other people sick. And you are not going to get
a lot out of these guys. You got to be disciplined when
discipline is needed. You know, when a guy is a screw-
off you got to discipline him. Then you go ahead and
you go all the way with this guy. . . . That's all you
need, talk. Well, I got some guys here that are tight.
Loosen up, man, get loose, come on. Sit down and talk
with your people. You're the manager. Talk with them.
Find out what's wrong with them. Don't say, "He's
stupid," or "I hate you." You are never going to get
nothing done like that. You can't tell a guy you hate
him. Find out why you hate him. Maybe he hates you
the same way. Iron your difference out, get that hate
out of you, man. Find out what it is. It could be
something that could be so simple to iron out.[12] ⫿⫿⫿

In developing a humane managerial touch, Angela Sealy,
who began her career as a rail clerk and finished as an assistant
train dispatcher, found that her favorite phrase with her co-
workers was "Can you do me a favor?"

⫿⫿⫿ And the girl who took my job, who I broke in for the job, I told her the same thing. I said, "They respect you and you respect them. They are human beings just like you are." I treated those people just the way I would like to be treated. That's how it worked and I found that it was very nice.[13] ⫿⫿⫿

CHAPTER 13

GENERATIONS

> There was no good old days. That's a lot of balo-
> ney. The only good thing about the good old days
> is I was ten, fifteen, twenty years younger. That's
> all that was good about it.
>
> *Joseph P. Fox*, Senior Railroad Signal Specialist[1]

Tew York City Transit workers often seem like an ex-
tended family united by the common experiences of
work. As in all families, there are differences between
generations. Transit workers' stories about themselves, their
forebears, and their descendants on the job reach back to the
Depression of the 1930s and look forward to the twenty-first
century. When transit workers talk about their different generations, they define their place in the ongoing history of their
work and establish the meaning of labor in their lives. And they
figure out who they are on the job.

"When you looked at them, they looked like ragbags," Mike
Lombardi recalls of his father's generation, which went into
Transit in the 1920s and 1930s.

▓▓ They used to have a motorman's cap or railroad cap squashed down, dungaree cap with a poppy in it, because everybody was patriotic.

They loved the country. Most of these guys came from countries where they had nothing. There's things wrong with America, but they loved it. Most of them were veterans. So they would wear poppies in their hat.

They all walked around with little pieces of cardboard, a little square of cardboard like from a matchbook. The reason for the cardboard was their buttonhole. . . . These guys are putting on weight, and the buttons would pop off. So what they would do is, they would stick this button to it, and put a piece of cardboard behind it.

Home-made tools. They had a tool with five wrench heads welded to the end of one. They used to call them Flintstone wrenches. They were very lazy. Why carry five wrenches?[2] ▓▓

Lombardi has risen far from his first transit job as a machinist's helper, but he knows too much about working life to romanticize it—especially when it comes to his father's generation of transit workers.

▓▓ We had a lost generation. My father went to college, and years ago that's quite an accomplishment. But he couldn't get a job during the Depression.

There was thousands and millions of people like this. They were very talented people who got lost. They got high school educations, which was fabulous back in the thirties. And there weren't jobs for them—for years. And they couldn't get married because they didn't have any work.

Just when they were getting married, World War II breaks out. And they all get drafted. They're in the war for five or six years. And when they come back there's no housing. And very talented people got stuck in places like the Transit Authority, because they were the only jobs.

So that's how my father ended up here. A very
talented guy, a composer, a writer. There were lots of
people like him—sculptors, artists, people with beautiful
talents.

And on top of that they were skilled: they were good
electricians—they had a lot of talent, just couldn't catch
a break, and they got stuck in the Transit Authority.

And had they been in our generation, they would
have really been something. They would have been able
to make a lot of money. They would have gotten the
fruits of their talent. They couldn't get it in those days,
because they were a lost generation.   ▥

Richie Triolo of the Lighting Department thinks about "old
school" transit workers and an image appears in his mind: a
man in coveralls, pockets full of pens, tools strung around his
waist, wearing a hat with a pencil in it.

▥   Their attitude was very gung-ho. "Do it my way."
And let's say you're the new kid in the block like I was,
"Do it my way or no way."

They were interesting, they were from the old
school. Most of them were in World War II. So they
were more disciplined. The young guys, they weren't
in the service so they had less discipline.

But the old-timers were born in the Depression. So
they were very grateful for the job and they didn't mind
working twelve hours a day.

And when they would go home, they changed their
clothes but they still had their work keys around their
waists. They were with eighteen pens and the little
tester, in case a guy walks out of the station and sees a
light out, "Let me see if the circuit is open or it's a
burnt-out bulb." The old-timers probably went to bed
at night with a flashlight and a helmet on.[3]   ▥

And some old-timers, as bus driver Fred McFarland recalls,
were great characters.

▥   I actually feel that the Scottish and the old Irish

guys and a lot of the black guys uptown, I mean they
made this job. I mean they came right off the boat and
they were either motormen or bus drivers and a lot of
them broke me in and 99 percent of them aren't here
anymore. There was one guy, Frank. . . . He was the
lover of the 132nd Street garage. He had a girlfriend in
every bus stop. He was training me and he says . . . "I
got to meet Maisie at Forty-second Street." So that's
where we would terminate, at Forty-second Street,
because he was meeting one of his girlfriends.[4] ∥∥∥

To younger transit workers who started out in the decades
after World War II, old-timers could be rivals or teachers. If
they were rivals, it was partly because younger men and older
men both wanted to work overtime to increase their paychecks.
Older workers, especially in repair yards, knew that if they kept
their mechanical skills to themselves, they would not have to
worry about younger workers taking over their jobs when
management offered overtime.[5]

In this rivalry, some young workers concluded that old-timers
were callously indifferent to their younger counterparts. John
Lorusso recalls,

∥∥∥   When I first started, I was a helper in the Repair
and Renewal Gang. I was working with this old-timer
at Fourteenth Street, and I was working oiling these
moving platforms that extend from the platform.

He says, "Hey, kid, go under there and oil these rods
here, and I'll watch for the trains."

And I'm oiling away, and all of a sudden I looked
and he had cleared up. He didn't tell me no train was
coming. I had to dive under the moving platform. I was
lucky that the one that I was oiling at that time happened to have a little space underneath, and I dove
under there and the train passed.

He says, "I thought I told you." He was one of those
real old-timers; I guess he was beyond his years. He
should have retired before then, but he didn't.

It took me a few days to be extracautious and look a little more, to look more for my safety. In other words, not rely on other people all the time.

But at that time I was new. I figured, Well, he's there, he's an old-timer, he knows what to do when a train comes. And he didn't, he just stepped away, and the train just kept coming.[6] ⅢⅢ

The silences between older and younger workers were sometimes the consequence of different ways of doing complex jobs. Where a younger worker might use a schematic diagram to wire a subway car, an older one would rely on memory and self-made reminders that might not work for someone else. Richard Buffington believes that some old-timers were reluctant to teach younger workers because it would expose the limits of their book knowledge.

ⅢⅢ A couple of times I worked with this one person in particular who I thought was a fantastic mechanic and he was. I asked him, "Hey, Mike, why don't you show me that on the schematic?"

"Later, later."

All right. I didn't pursue it, because I found out later on that he really didn't know how to read a schematic.

A lot of guys had books, little butcher books, they called them. And they would put down car numbers and what was wrong with a car. They wrote it in their own way, like a dead motor in second point, a dead motor in first point. And they put down the symptom and the remedy. And then if they ran into another problem where it was a different remedy, they'd also put that in until they would get a nice book, a little reference library for them.

Basically they really didn't have the ability to translate their knowledge to you because their way of troubleshooting was through trial and error and there was no way to communicate that to somebody else.

And I think they were embarrassed too. They would

say, "Go get me this. I'll show you some other time."
And everybody felt that when you were going away to
get the part, they were fixing the thing up.[7] ⅢⅢ

Younger workers found ways of getting even. Lloyd Tyler
remembers:

ⅢⅢ We had one guy, he was sharp but he would do all
the wiring by memory or bending a wire this way or
that way so he could remember what it was. And there
was a wise guy that found out his system and changed
the wires. Drove this guy batty. Because, see, if you go
by a schematic or wire diagram it doesn't matter. You
can always take the wire diagram out, wire A goes to
wire B, wire C to D, so forth. But if you go by
memory or your own little code, if somebody messes it
up you are shot.[8] ⅢⅢ

But despite such rivalries, according to Jeffrey Van Clief,
there were offers to share the skills of the trade. Out of such
encounters, young transit workers gathered the wisdom of their
predecessors. John Lorusso recalls,

ⅢⅢ There's Leo Makarowski. He was a big, strapping
guy. He was a signalman. He helped me quite a bit.
Andy Angus was another big, strapping guy. He helped
me quite a bit. They'd look after you. They'd show you
the easy ways to do something. Willy Gordon was one
of my first maintainers. He showed me a lot. He helped
me in one way, and I helped him in another way.
Because at that time, there was a transition going on
with the signal equipment, and he was used to the old
equipment and he was a little—not old—but he was set
in his ways, where he didn't pick up as fast on the
newer stuff. At that time, I was young and ambitious,
and I picked up the new stuff and taught him. And he
showed me the old stuff. A lot of times, instinctively,
he'd know what was wrong. He'd just go to a certain
area that we'd had trouble on, and he'd be able to tell

you what the trouble was before you even looked for it.
It goes with time, you know. ⅢⅢ

When Mike Lombardi recalls an old work injury, he relates
not just the callousness of a foreman and doctor who asked him
to continue working in pain, but also the canny remedy offered
by an old-style German mechanic.

ⅢⅢ I broke my toe once. I dropped something on my
toe. About a forty- or fifty-pound thing. I don't have
steel-tipped shoes on.

And it hits my toe, and I can think of nothing except
my toe. There's nothing else in life that's happening or
going on. There's nothing more important than the
pain in this toe. I can't walk. They put me on a high-
low, a forklift type of thing, and they're driving me to
the clinic. And the pain, I can't believe it. My big toe is
beating like a heart. Boomp, boomp, boomp. I can't
even take my shoe off, you know. It's unbelievable.

I'm going by the machine shop, and a little German
guy comes out. Most of the machinists were Germans.
They were all Fritzes and Hanses. And Hans comes out
says, "Let's look at your toe."

So I says, "Oh my God, I dropped this thing on my
toe."

"Well, come in here. Come into the tool room. I'll
drill holes in your toenails, and it will relieve your—"

"Hey, Hans, you screwball, I'm not coming in, I'm
going to the doctor. No, Hans, a machinist knows how
to work with machines. Your toe is broken you go to a
doctor, you don't go to the machinist, right? Mur-
derer." And he's crazy, you know. "Get away from me,
Hans."

"No, I'll drill a few holes in your toe." I had visions
of the drill press getting stuck and going right through
my toe.

"Get lost, Hans."

So I go to the clinic and they point an X ray, and my

toe is beating like a heart. . . . And the doctor says,
"OK, restricted duty."

Restricted duty: work. I got to get out of here. I
want to go home. It should be *no* work, not restricted. I
can't work. What—restricted? I can't think. I can't sit.
"You didn't even look at my toe." He didn't even look
at it. "So why didn't you look at my toe? You're a
doctor. The machinist wanted to look at my toe. You
don't want to look at my toe." He says, "Well, you've
seen one broken toe, you've seen them all." That's
exactly what he said to me.

So I said to him, "Yeah, but this toe is on *my* foot.
This is part of *my* body. You gotta look at this toe." I
said, "The whole nail is filled with blood. It's killing
me. It's beating like—what am I to do?"

"It's restricted duty—work."

I go back to my foreman, he says, "I'm sorry, you
can't go home."

I says, "Get lost. I'm going home. The doctor didn't
even look at my toe."

"Well, you know, you can't leave, you'll be
AWOL—"

"I'm going home." I went home.

Someone stepped on my toe on the way home, and
about eight at night I can't take it anymore. I don't
want to go to a doctor. You know, I just don't want to
go to a doctor. But I can't take it anymore, and the pain
brings me to the doctor.

The doctor says, "Put your foot over here." And he
took out a scalpel and he drilled three holes in my nail
like Hans would. I should have gone to Hans, it
wouldn't have cost me fifteen dollars.

He drilled three holes in my nail, and all the blood
came out, and that was the end. No pain. Hans was
right. The machinist was right.   ⅢⅢⅢ

Sometimes, the lesson from the older generation to the
younger was an exercise in attitude. Old-timers measured them-

selves by their ability to do their work, no matter how hard or
heavy. If a train broke down, veteran train operators took it as
a personal insult, recalls Jeffrey Van Clief.

‖‖‖ Most of the time these guys would call up and say,
"I'm laying down, I'm at such and such a place, I'm
laying down, I got an air brake leak." Boom. Hang up.

By the time you got there, walked to this train, this
guy was back in charging it up, ready to go. You holler,
"What happened?"

He says, "What are you doing here, lad?"

"I've come to fix your train."

"No, lad, get off my train, the train is all right, lad, I
don't need you."

Because the pride was there. He didn't want to feel
embarrassed that he had to have help. He'd fix it
himself.

I remember one time up in Broadway, one day I'm
in the pit and I'm working on a controller and I hear,
"Pull, Martin, pull." So I think, "What is Martin
pulling?"

They got a rope around a train and they're pulling it
into the shop by hand. So, I come out of the pit.

They say, "Here's a young lad, a healthy young lad.
Come here, lad. Grab a-hold of the rope and pull.
What's your name?"

"Jeff."

"Pull, Jeff; pull, Martin."

I'm pulling with these guys.

"God damn, lad, no wonder we lost the Korean
War, you're not pulling. Pull! Pull! Pull! Pull! Pull!"

We got the train in. I said, "Why didn't you wait for
a motorman?"

"We haven't got time for a motorman, lad. We got
to get this train. People are waiting for this train. We
got to make service this afternoon."

Different type of a person. If you tell someone today
to pull a train in, the union would come after them

with handcuffs, take you out somewhere, and shoot you. ⫾⫾⫾

In the 1990s, the old-time transit workers who went on the job in the 1930s and 1940s are long gone from the Transit Authority. The 1968 transit workers' contract allowed them to retire after twenty years at half pay if they were fifty years old or more. The contract has been revised since, but its initial effect was to give many old-timers an opportunity to retire into relative comfort. Time passed, more retired. Today, the very oldest transit workers—workers in their sixties on the brink of retirement—are people who started working in the 1950s.

From the security of retirement, the oldest old-timers evaluate their successors. Charles E. Smith, who in 1942 became one of the first African American bus drivers hired in New York City, looks on in dismay.

⫾⫾⫾ When we started on the bus, the pay was sixty-seven cents an hour. I recall telling my wife, "Maybe if I can get a job making twenty-five dollars a week, we got it made." My wife never worked. What are the young fellas making today? They're making sixteen dollars and something an hour. And you're getting less service. They have an attitude. Do you ride buses occasionally? Do you see the appearance of some of these bus drivers, the way they look in their uniform? And they don't have to buy them, all they have to do is maintain them, keep them clean and pressed.

You go into any job—they seem to think that *you* owe them a living. It's your business, now you hire me, then when I start to working for you I feel as if you're *supposed* to hire me, and it's your business. That's the attitude of the average bus driver. Attitudes have changed completely since World War II. Big breakdown in morals of all ethnic groups. They feel that the world owes them a living. They don't want to use their brains.[9] ⫾⫾⫾

Senior transit workers, younger than the generation that

started work before or during World War II but still influenced
by their example, can be amazed by the attitudes of even younger
workers. Jeffrey Van Clief, who started to work in Transit in
1958, is one of them.

⫼ The attitude today is that we got spoiled kids. I'll
give you a good example. My kid is spoiled. My kid
was offered a job here as a car cleaner and he said, "I
ain't cleaning toilets."
Most of the people I knew when I came in were
from '47 back to 1918. They were altogether different.
They seen a lot of hard times. I was given a lot of
advice.
One advice I never forget was given by a man named
George O'Connor. He went through the Depression
while working for the Transit Authority. And he told
me one day, "Whatever they do, kid, if you ever go
through a Depression in the City of New York, never
quit this job. Take a cut in pay, take a demotion. But
you'll have a job. Don't ever feel that they're going to
do something to your character, that they're demeaning
you. You've got something to feed your family with. I
mean, stick it out. It's got to get better before it gets
worse." ⫼

But a young man's expectations of work, shaped by the decades of prosperity that followed World War II, cannot be compared fairly to the expectations of men who went to work in
the shadow of the Great Depression. As the Transit Authority
modernizes its operations and brings in new managers, seniority is no guarantee of expertise or security today. Some older
workers feel that their hard-won knowledge is ignored. Marty
Kaiser, a general superintendent who started with the Transit
Authority as a helper in 1955, feels the pinch.

⫼ I've walked all of the tracks in every division, I've
been to every station in every division, I've walked
through every river tube, all of the car barns I've been
in, and the bus garages. So if you talk to me about

something, I can close my eyes, I don't even have to
close my eyes, just talking with you now I can think of
a place and I can see that place.

And I don't think a new person coming in can see
that. OK, they're good mechanics, but I don't think
there's really anything like experience.

You need new blood, but you also need the old
blood with it too, to tell the new blood, "Watch out
for this" or "There's a problem with that" or "If you
get in this little bind, this is what you should do."

To me, there's nothing like experience. That's what
I believe anyhow. Maybe because I'm getting older
now.[10] ▥

But Paul Prinzivalli, who also went into transit after World
War II and went from being a track worker to an instructor,
welcomes new blood into the Transit workforce.

▥   A lot of people resent people from other railroads
coming in. I like it. They're coming in with new ideas.
We're generating into more modernized, mechanized
equipment. It's making our jobs more professional-like,
rather than the common laborer pick-and-shovel. And
they believe in training, they're much more educated
than the old group.

The old group came up from hard knocks, they
didn't have college education, and education is an
important factor in generating policies. This new group,
all I can say is compliments to them. Because their ideas
did change our railroad standards in work output.[11] ▥

Older and younger generations of transit workers often live
in the same family. Mike Lombardi's father lived long enough
to see Mike rise to supervisor, which gave the father great pride.
Lombardi also recalls how transit supervisors use family con-
nections to maintain discipline among younger workers.

▥   We have a lot of kids at work, young guys.
Twenty-one, nineteen, twenty-two years old—they're

not kids, but we call them kids. They're old enough to
die in a war, but we can call them kids, right?

But anyway, they're the sons of the mothers and
fathers that worked here. A lot of kids follow in their
parents' footsteps, a lot of kids come, their uncles
worked here, or their brother worked here, their father
worked here. And most of their parents were supervisors and members of management. And they're starting
their way up, from helper, all the way up. And they're
rambunctious, and full of hell, and when they step out
of line, it's interesting, we don't want to call their
fathers, because it's embarrassing, the father may have
retired; the last thing a good supervisor wants when he
retires is to get a phone call that his son is not perform-
ing well on the job.

We have a guy here, Joe Deluca, who's an interesting character. He's a superintendent, and he knows all
these young guys. And we tolerate some of their stuff
and we put them in their place when necessary, and we
direct their energies and their anger and all this stuff
toward the job. We get them squared away.

But the best thing is that Joe goes shopping on the
weekends and he lives in the same neighborhood as
these kids and he always bumps into their mothers. And
their mothers are saying, "Hiya Joe, howya doing?
How's my son Frankie doing?"

"Well, um, Frankie's not doing so good, you know;
Frankie's fooling around at work."

"What!"

"Yeah."

"Why didn't you tell us before?"

"We don't want to embarrass the father; we'll tell
you."

"Did you discipline him for it?"

Well, we don't want to discipline. We don't want to
hurt their records. We want to change their behavior.
We don't want to stigmatize them for the rest of their

life here. You know, we have a little compassion for
them. Because they really aren't bad. We want to
change their behavior. We can't change their behavior,
you know, it's tough.

So, we let their mothers change their behavior. The
mother says to them at dinner time, when the father's
not around, "Hey, what do you want, to lose this job?"
Because the mother's so happy he's got the job: he's
secure, he's got his pension, he's got medical benefits,
he's got dental plans, he's got drug plans, he's got
vacations, he's doing very well. And the mothers talk to
them and they come back the next day walking a
straight line. ⅢⅢ

Ultimately, the dialogue between generations of transit workers is not a debate between superior seniors and inferior young
people. As Lombardi notes of the transit generations, "You had
a group of people who were very uneducated. Uneducated but
intelligent. No formal training, but smart. Then you had a group
that had formal education and talent, and then you had us kids
that had a decent education and no talent."

Instead, it is a conversation in which American workers born
in different eras with different needs and expectations try to
define their own lives and work by comparing themselves to
other workers. If the conclusions are incomplete, that is because the process of making and remaking the American working class never stops. As Joseph P. Fox sees it,

ⅢⅢ   I mean, the good old days had their problems. The
sixties were very turbulent. We had a social revolution
going on in this country. We were in the Vietnam War.

In the fifties we were worrying about the Russians.
Kennedy got in. We had the window of vulnerability
with nuclear war.

My whole life there's been bad and good in every
day that I've lived. I don't know that there is such a
thing as good old days. If you ask me, these are the
good old days. ⅢⅢ

CHAPTER 14

INTO THE FUTURE

> It is a good job, it is truly a good job. It is a
> fulfilling job if you take the job to heart. We do a
> job that no one else can do, and I feel quite proud
> of that.
>
> *Anthony Santella*, Maintenance Supervisor[1]

T he end of a career in Transit can be a time for taking
stock of the years. When the time came for Scotty
McShane to retire, he was reminded of the friends he
made driving a bus.

‖‖‖‖ I had one of my passengers just recently say to me,
"Did you make up your mind when you're going to
retire?"

I says, "Yeah, December 21 I'm leaving."

I knew her about fifteen years, she says to me,
"Where do I write the letter to stop it?"

So I said, "Stop what?"

She says, "You can't leave us." She says, "Who we
going to get in your place?"

I says, "Another driver."

She says, "Oh no, I'll write," she says, "I know some people. I'll write a letter to stop your retirement."

I says, "But I want to retire. I want out." But this is regular passengers. You get to know these people; they're your buddies, they're your good friends.[2] ⦚

The friendships made in Transit can loom large in a worker's assessment of the job. Richard Buffington says,

⦚ You get to know people here more than your family because you're here eight hours a day, traveling time to get here and half the time you meet people in the subway that you're working with or you go home with them. And then when you are home you're not really with your family as much as you are with the people here. In a way it becomes your family, this place, you know. Then it's hard to see some people that you really respected and you liked and you worked with and you find out the guy passed on or something else happened to him. That's the only sad part.[3] ⦚

Part of the gratification at the end of a career comes from knowing that you helped other people make careers of their own. Angela Sealy cherishes a letter dated August 3, 1990, from a woman, Janet Aaron, whom she directed to the right job in Transit.

⦚ This thank-you note is long overdue. Your kindness and thoughtfulness has affected my life and family. . . . I can tell you this, you really know your job. The way you place people in jobs who live in Brooklyn and the Bronx, you showed your kindness and understanding of what we have to go through. You knew who could do the job and who could not. This helped keep a lot of us out of serious trouble. You are very much loved out here on the road. One more thing, I can really say you have a wonderful memory. All I can say is I'm glad I have known you. Angela, have a happy retirement. You will always be in my thoughts.[4] ⦚

Thomas Granger, one of the early African American drivers on the Fifth Avenue Coach buses, enjoys knowing that he helped others get jobs in Transit.

⫼ To be honest with you, the real feeling I get that I have accomplished something is when I get on the buses now, some of the old-timers are there. I had one bus driver stop me in the middle of Edgecombe Avenue . . . he had a busload of people. He said, "Mr. Granger!"

I knew the face, I said, "How do you do, buddy?"

He said, "Nineteen years. I put two kids through college."

That's the reward that I get, the feeling that I've accomplished something. . . . I used to teach the operators on my own, black operators mostly but it was open to anybody, we had a little school, if you'd come we'd tell you how to pass the test to become a supervisor, we'd tell you the questions that's going to be asked, and how you have to prepare an answer, we really schooled them. And guys that came to the school, they all passed.[5] ⫼

The transit workers who retire today leave behind an evolving system. If they arrived in the shadow of the old IRT, they leave a system that is growing more complex technically and whose managerial practices are changing. Some workers believe that newer managerial styles, and an emphasis on formal education and training, undercut the human factors that can make the system reliable.

Conductor Jim Miles thinks that the idiosyncrasies of the system need to be taken into account.

⫼ The New York City subway is a railroad. It is such a large-scale railroad that there are a lot of things to take into account, there's a lot to it in running it. Somebody comes along and tries to apply a science to it and thinks that science is going to work. In other words, it works fine on paper but practically it doesn't work. And that's basically what's happening. They are trying to make the Transit Authority and the running of this railroad like some kind of, how can I put it, almost like a factory, like the running of a factory where you have set times to do this, this, this, and this. Like the schedules that we have, it would work nice if we could keep to those schedules by the second but there are too many things that happen to throw it off.[6]   ‖‖

Mike Lombardi balances frustration and pride when he looks back over the years.

‖‖   You know, I was always going to quit the place. This is paradoxical. Although I didn't like this place, I didn't want the day to end quickly. This is hard to believe, but like, on a Friday, I used to watch the clock, and it was moving too quickly. Four o'clock was coming around too soon. It was going-home time. And I really didn't want to go home. I wanted bigger and better things for myself, so I was dissatisfied there. But as far as the actual job was concerned, I liked being with the people, all the characters, because we had very talented people here.[7]   ‖‖

Lombardi looks back on an unusual trajectory: East New York Vocational and Technical High School to community college to helper, machinist helper, and then on up to Chief of Service Delivery. "It's, like, only in America," he concludes.

‖‖   It's very interesting, it's changed a lot. It's exciting. There's always something. It's not humdrum. You're doing a lot of different things every day and you feel like you're doing something because there's a couple of million people out there every day depending on us.   ‖‖

At the most basic level, transit workers depend on their jobs to pay the bills; the city depends on transit workers to run the largest bus and subway system in the nation. But often, as we've heard, work is more than just a job.

New York City is portrayed as a place where everyone is a

stranger, but transit workers provide a human presence on a late-night bus or an empty subway platform. New York City is depicted as a place where people relentlessly pursue selfish interests, but transit workers labor daily on subway tracks inches from high-voltage power lines, risking their lives for passengers whose names they never know. New York City is thought to be so big and so fragmented that its people have nothing in common, but the buses and subways that transit workers command create common threads in the lives of all New Yorkers.

207th Street yard with IND cars lined up for the evening.
PHOTOGRAPH COURTESY OF THE NEW YORK TRANSIT MUSEUM.

NOTES

1. Whitfield Lee interview with Sally Charnow, New York, New York, 21 August 1989.
2. "Cumulative Workforce Analysis, New York City Transit, as of July 31, 1997," MTA/New York City Transit, Department of Affirmative Action, EEO, and Business Programs, Division of Equal Employment Authority.
3. Paul Fussell, *Class: A Guide to the American Status System* (New York: Summit Books, 1983), 25–26.
4. Raymond Berger interview with Joseph Sciorra, New York, New York, 10 October 1990.
5. These ideas were developed in Joshua B. Freeman, "The Long Ride to Justice," *New York Newsday*, 26 February 1993, 56.

1. Lionel Bostick interview with Sally Charnow, New York, New York, 14 May 1989.
2. Joe Caracciolo interview with Sally Charnow, New York, New York, 24 July 1989.
3. Roland Shelton interview with Sally Charnow, New York, New York, 30 August 1989.
4. Jeffrey Van Clief interview with Joseph Sciorra, New York, New York, 30 October 1990.
5. Paul Prinzivalli interview with Sally Charnow and Ray Allen, New York, New York, 27 July 1989.
6. Joseph Tesoriero interview with Sally Charnow, New York, New York, 21 July 1989.

1. Joseph Allotta interview with Sally Charnow, New York, New York, 30 August 1989.

2. John Maye interview with Sally Charnow, New York, New York, 25 August 1989.

3. Richie Triolo interview with Joseph Sciorra, New York, New York, 9 November 1990; Victor De Santo interview with Joseph Sciorra, New York, New York, 25 October 1990.

4. Whitfield Lee interview with Sally Charnow, New York, New York, 21 August 1989.

5. Carol Meltzer interview with Sally Charnow, New York, New York, 5 December 1990.

6. Don Harold interview with Sally Charnow, New York, New York, 26 July 1989.

7. Mildred Hunter interview with Sally Charnow, New York, New York, 18 July 1989.

8. Mike Lombardi and Joe Fernandez interview with Sally Charnow, New York, New York, 1 September 1989.

9. Joe Caracciolo interview with Sally Charnow, New York, New York, 24 July 1989.

10. Joseph Tesoriero interview with Sally Charnow, New York, New York, 21 July 1989.

11. Brenda Hayes interview with Sally Charnow, New York, New York, 12 December 1990.

12. George Havriliak interview with Sally Charnow, New York, New York, 30 September 1989.

13. [Dick Hinton, pseud.] interview with Joseph Sciorra, New York, New York, 30 October 1990.

⁞⁞⁞⁞⁞ 3. STATIONS AND FARES

1. Whitfield Lee interview with Sally Charnow, New York, New York, 21 August 1989.

2. Jeffrey Van Clief interview with Joseph Sciorra, New York, New York, 30 October 1990.

3. Carol Meltzer interview with Sally Charnow, New York, New York, 5 December 1990.

4. Brenda Hayes interview with Sally Charnow, New York, New York, 12 December 1990.

5. On railroad clerk and booth robberies, see Jim Dwyer, *Subway Lives: 24 Hours in the Life of the New York City Subway* (New York: Crown, 1991), 25–29.

6. John Waddell and Rosalyn Samuels interview with Sally Charnow, New York, New York, 13 September 1989.

7. Lionel Bostick interview with Sally Charnow, New York, New York, 14 May 1989.

⁞⁞⁞⁞⁞ 4. OPERATING TRAINS

1. Stanley Stern interview with Sally Charnow, New York, New York, 14 September 1989.

2. On the Malbone Street wreck, see Clifton Hood, *722 Miles: The Building of the Subways and How They Transformed New York* (New York: Simon and Schuster, 1993), 190–193; also Brian J. Cudahy, *Under the Sidewalks of New York: The Story of the World's Greatest Subway System* (New York: The Stephen Greene Press, Pelham Books, 1979, 1989), 75–77.

3. Joe Cassar interview with Joseph Sciorra, New York, New York, 11 October 1990.

4. Joseph P. Fox interview with Sally Charnow, New York, New York, 24 August 1989.

5. Robert Kolacz interview with Sally Charnow, New York, New York, 12 December 1990.

6. Ed Krieger interview with Sally Charnow, New York, New York, 22 September 1989.

7. [Jim Miles, pseud.] interview with Joseph Sciorra, New York, New York, 21 January 1991.

8. Harry Nugent interview with Sally Charnow, New York, New York, 12 November 1990.

‖‖‖ 5. SIX INCHES FROM DEATH

1. Jenny Mandelino interview with Sally Charnow, New York, New York, 15 August 1989.

2. Joe Caracciolo interview with Sally Charnow, New York, New York, 24 July 1989.

3. John Lorusso interview with Sally Charnow, New York, New York, 31 August 1989.

4. Harry Nugent interview with Sally Charnow, New York, New York, 12 November 1990.

5. Richard Oakes interview with Sally Charnow, New York, New York, 24 July 1989.

6. Paul Prinzivalli interview with Sally Charnow and Ray Allen, New York, New York, 27 July 1989.

7. Marty Kaiser interview with Sally Charnow, New York, New York, 20 July 1989.

8. Richard Oakes; Earnis Briant interview with Sally Charnow, New York, New York, 17 August 1989.

9. Eric Schmidt interview with Sally Charnow, New York, New York, 24 July 1989.

10. Emilio Robertino interview with Sally Charnow, New York, New York, 24 July 1989.

11. Joseph P. Fox interview with Sally Charnow, New York, New York, 24 July 1989.

12. Richie Triolo interview with Joseph Sciorra, New York, New York, 9 November 1990.

13. Lionel Bostick interview with Sally Charnow, New York, New York, 14 May 1989.

‖‖‖   6. LAW AND ORDER

1. John Maye interview with Sally Charnow, New York, New York, 25 August 1989.
2. Carolyn Burke interview with Sally Charnow, New York, New York, 30 August 1990.
3. Richard Marks interview with Sally Charnow, New York, New York, 5 September 1989.
4. Floyd Holloway interview with Sally Charnow, New York, New York, 23 August 1989.
5. On crime reductions, see *The Case Against Merger* (Metropolitan Transit Authority, 1994), 5–6. On morale, see Paul D. May, "Bratton Gave Us Pride. Must We Give It Back?" *New York Newsday*, 6 June 1994, A24.

‖‖‖   7. DRIVING BUSES

1. Fred McFarland and Scotty McShane interview with Joseph Sciorra, New York, New York, 31 October 1990.
2. [Dick Hinton, pseud.] interview with Joseph Sciorra, New York, New York, 30 October 1990.

‖‖‖   8. SHOPS AND YARDS

1. Mike Lombardi and Joe Fernandez interview with Sally Charnow, New York, New York, 1 September 1989.
2. George Havriliak interview with Sally Charnow, New York, New York, 30 September 1989.
3. Vincent Ricciardelli and James Davitt interview with Sally Charnow, New York, New York, 7 December 1990.
4. Leonard Offner interview with Joseph Sciorra, New York, New York, 11 October 1990.
5. Joseph Allotta interview with Sally Charnow, New York, New York, 30 August 1989.
6. A. R. Goodlatte interview with Susan Brophy, New York, New York, 25 August 1988.
7. Richard Buffington interview with Joseph Sciorra, New York, New York, 25 October 1990.

‖‖‖   9. MATTERS OF COLOR

1. Emilio Robertino interview with Sally Charnow, New York, New York, 24 July 1989.
2. For the statistics, see "Cumulative Workforce Analysis, New York City Transit, as of July 31, 1997"; for the relative success of the integration of the transit workforce as compared to the private sector, see Joshua B. Freeman, "The Long Ride to Justice," *New York Newsday*, 26 February 1993, 56.
3. Fred McFarland and Scotty McShane interview with Joseph Sciorra, New York, New York, 31 October 1990.

4. Penny Rohls interview with Sally Charnow, New York, New York, 21 August 1989.

5. Lionel Bostick interview with Sally Charnow, New York, New York, 14 May 1989.

6. For a brief account of the integration of the transit workforce, see Freeman, "The Long Ride to Justice," 56; also see Joshua B. Freeman, *In Transit: The Transport Workers Union in New York City, 1933–1966* (New York: Oxford University Press, 1989), 151–154.

7. See Cheryl Lynn Greenberg, *"Or Does It Explode?": Black Harlem in the Great Depression* (New York: Oxford University Press, 1991), 204.

8. See Greenberg, *"Or Does It Explode?"* 204–205; Charles V. Hamilton, *Adam Clayton Powell, Jr.: The Political Biography of an American Dilemma* (New York: Atheneum, 1991), 102–103; and Freeman, "The Long Ride to Justice."

9. Charles E. Smith interview with Sally Charnow, New York, New York, 12 July 1989.

10. Thomas Granger interview with Sally Charnow, New York, New York, 30 June 1989.

11. Marty Kaiser interview with Sally Charnow, New York, New York, 20 July 1989.

12. Albert Schneider interview with Joseph Sciorra, New York, New York, 9 January 1991.

13. Lloyd Tyler, James Daniels, and Jean Frugone interview with Joseph Sciorra, New York, New York, 8 November 1990.

14. Earnis Briant interview with Sally Charnow, New York, New York, 17 August 1989.

15. Samuel Zelensky interview with Sally Charnow, New York, New York, 7 November 1989.

16. Frances Murphy interview with Sally Charnow, New York, New York, 29 June 1989.

‖‖ 10. WORK, WOMEN, AND MEN

1. Elena Chang interview with Sally Charnow, New York, New York, 26 July 1989.

2. Shirley Thaler and Diane Leibovitz interview with Sally Charnow, New York, New York, 15 October 1990.

3. Theodore Jones and Joey Deher interview with Joseph Sciorra, New York, New York, 11 October 1990.

4. Joseph P. Fox interview with Sally Charnow, New York, New York, 24 August 1989.

5. Mike Lombardi and Joe Fernandez interview with Sally Charnow, New York, New York, 1 September 1989.

6. Penny Rohls interview with Sally Charnow, New York, New York, 21 August 1989.

7. Jenny Mandelino interview with Sally Charnow, New York, New York, 15 August 1989.

8. Diane Leibovitz and Shirley Thaler interview with Sally Charnow, New York, New York, 15 October 1990.

9. Brenda Hayes interview with Sally Charnow, New York, New York, 12 December 1990.

10. Jeffrey Van Clief interview with Joseph Sciorra, New York, New York, 30 October 1990.

⠿ 11. UNION TALK

1. Stanley Stern interview with Sally Charnow, New York, New York, 14 September 1989.

2. On work conditions in pre-union mass transit, see Joshua B. Freeman, *In Transit: The Transport Workers Union in New York City, 1933–1966* (New York: Oxford University Press, 1989), 10–15 (for the death see p. 14); on bent backs and curled hands, see Victor De Santo interview with Joseph Sciorra, New York, New York, 25 October 1990.

3. For an assessment of Local 100 in 1996, see "New Blood Brings Union New Life," *Newsday*, 21 March 1996, A2.

4. Freeman, *In Transit*, 5–6. For the quote, see Marty Kaiser interview with Sally Charnow, New York, New York, 20 July 1989.

5. Tim Griffin interview, cited in Joseph Doyle, "The Controversial History of the TWU," *The New York Irish* (1986), 8.

6. John O'Brien interview with Brenda Parnes, 26 April 1988, Tamiment Collection, New York University.

7. Doyle, "The Controversial History of the TWU," 8–9.

8. Victor De Santo.

9. Mike Lombardi and Joe Fernandez interview with Sally Charnow, New York, New York, 1 September 1989.

10. Joseph Allotta interview with Sally Charnow, New York, New York, 30 August 1989.

11. On the strike and Quill's funeral, see Freeman, *In Transit*, 335.

12. See "T.W.U. Head Tells Queens Judge Transit Walkout Had to Be Ended," *New York Times*, 23 April 1980, B3.

13. "Discord in Union Is Seen as Posing Problem in Talks," *New York Times*, 7 April 1980, B1; also "Transit Worker Dissidents Predict a Rejection of Pact," *New York Times*, 13 April 1980, 34.

14. On the racial and ethnic composition of the Transit workforce, see "Cumulative Workforce Analysis, New York City Transit, as of July 31, 1997."

15. "Transit Union Dissidents Feel Pressure," *New York Times*, 15 October 1996, B3. Also see "Union Head Re-elected," *Newsday*, Queens edition, 17 December 1997, A28.

16. On various disputes between the union and management over the years, see "Cost-of-Living Raise for Transit Workers Is Attacked by Koch," *New York Times*, 21 October 1981, A1; "M.T.A. Seeks Modifications in Work Rules," *New York Times*, 8 April 1985, B1; "Safety First, Discipline Later," *New York Newsday*, 21 March 1991, 8; "Transit Union Head to Seek Strike

Approval," *New York Times*, 15 April 1992, B1; "Workers Say Trains Need Two Operators," *New York Times*, 2 July 1994, 23; and "Tentative Agreement Reached Between Union and M.T.A.," *New York Times*, 26 July 1994, B3. On divisions within Local 100, see "Transit Pact Is Approved by Workers," *New York Times*, 23 October 1996, B1.

17. On the workfare dispute, see "Transit Pact Is Approved by Workers," *New York Times*, 23 October 1996, B1; "Transit Union Agrees to Allow Workfare Plan," *New York Times*, 19 September 1996, A1; "Giuliani's Stand Thwarts Subway Workfare Plan," *New York Times*, 12 March 1997, B3; also "Too Few Welfare Workers, So Battle Becomes Tougher," *Daily News*, 5 May 1997, 6.

18. Vincent Ricciardelli and James Davitt interview with Sally Charnow, New York, New York, 7 December 1990.

19. Whitfield Lee interview with Sally Charnow, New York, New York, 21 August 1989.

20. See "New Blood Brings Union New Life," *Newsday*, 21 March 1996, A2.

21. Lionel Bostick interview with Sally Charnow, New York, New York, 14 May 1989.

⸿ 12. MOVING INTO MANAGEMENT

1. Emilio Robertino interview with Sally Charnow, New York, New York, 24 July 1989.

2. Richard Oakes interview with Sally Charnow, New York, New York, 24 July 1989.

3. Whitfield Lee interview with Sally Charnow, New York, New York, 21 August 1989.

4. Joseph Allotta interview with Sally Charnow, New York, New York, 30 August 1989.

5. Marty Kaiser interview with Sally Charnow, New York, New York, 20 July 1989.

6. Thomas Granger interview with Sally Charnow, New York, New York, 30 June 1989.

7. Mike Lombardi and Joe Fernandez interview with Sally Charnow, New York, New York, 1 September 1989.

8. Carol Meltzer interview with Sally Charnow, New York, New York, 5 December 1990.

9. Joseph P. Fox interview with Sally Charnow, New York, New York, 24 August 1989.

10. Stanley Stern interview with Sally Charnow, New York, New York, 14 September 1989.

11. Brenda Hayes interview with Sally Charnow, New York, New York, 12 December 1990.

12. Jeffrey Van Clief interview with Joseph Sciorra, New York, New York, 30 October 1990.

13. Angela Sealy interview with Joseph Sciorra, New York, New York, 9 January 1991.

‖‖‖ 13. GENERATIONS

1. Joseph P. Fox interview with Sally Charnow, New York, New York, 24 August 1989.

2. Mike Lombardi and Joe Fernandez interview with Sally Charnow, New York, New York, 1 September 1989.

3. Richie Triolo interview with Joseph Sciorra, New York, New York, 9 November 1990.

4. Fred McFarland and Scotty McShane interview with Joseph Sciorra, New York, New York, 31 October 1990.

5. On overtime and disputes between generations of workers, see James Davitt and Vincent Ricciardelli interview with Sally Charnow, New York, New York, 7 December 1990, and Lombardi.

6. John Lorusso interview with Sally Charnow, New York, New York, 31 August 1989.

7. Richard Buffington interview with Joseph Sciorra, New York, New York, 25 October 1990.

8. Lloyd Tyler, James Daniels, and Jean Frugone interview with Joseph Sciorra, New York New York, 8 November 1990.

9. Charles E. Smith interview with Sally Charnow, New York, New York, 12 May 1989.

10. Marty Kaiser interview with Sally Charnow, New York, New York, 20 July 1989.

11. Paul Prinzivalli interview with Sally Charnow and Ray Allen, New York, New York, 27 July 1989.

‖‖‖ 14. INTO THE FUTURE

1. Anthony Santella interview with Sally Charnow, New York, New York, 31 August 1989.

2. Scotty McShane and Fred McFarland interview with Joseph Sciorra, New York, New York, 31 October 1990.

3. Richard Buffington interview with Joseph Sciorra, New York, New York, 25 October 1990.

4. Angela Sealy interview with Joseph Sciorra, New York, New York, 9 January 1991.

5. Thomas Granger interview with Sally Charnow, New York, New York, 30 June 1989.

6. [Jim Miles, pseud.] interview with Joseph Sciorra, New York, New York, 21 January 1991.

7. Mike Lombardi and Joe Fernandez interview with Sally Charnow, New York, New York, 1 September 1989.

INDEX

ABOUT THE AUTHOR

Robert W. Snyder, a native New Yorker and the grandson of a transit worker, is a historian with a special interest in New York City. He is the author of *The Voice of the City: Vaudeville and Popular Culture in New York* and a co-author of *Metropolitan Lives: The Ashcan Artists and Their New York*, which won the Alfred H. Barr Prize of the College Art Association. He holds a doctorate in American history from New York University and is editor of *Media Studies Journal*.